OUR THANKS TO:
OUR FRIENDS FOR THEIR HELP AND RIUS WHO
SHOWED US THE WAY.

RUSSIAN REVOLUTIONARY CALENDAR

1789-94. The French Revolution.

1812. Napoleon's invasion of Russia and defeat. Described in Tolstoy's **War and Peace** (1869).

1825. The Decembrist Revolt against Tsarism.

1848. **The Communist Manifesto** by Marx and Engels appears on the eve of European revolution.

1861. Tsar Alexander II abolishes serfdom. Rise of **Narodism** - or 'peasant socialism' among radical intelligentsia.

1862-63. Formation of Narodnik underground movement **Zemlya i Volya** inspired by Chernyshevsky.

1864. The **First International** founded in London by Marx and others.

1869. Nechayev, Narodnik disciple of the anarchist Bakunin, prescribes terrorism.

1870. Birth of Lenin. Franco-Prussian War. Marx forecasts the Russian revolution.

1871. The Paris Commune.

1872. End of the First International in Europe. Russian translation of Marx's **Capital.** Dostoyevsky's **The Possessed.**

1874. The Narodnik "**going to the people**" movement suppressed by the Tsarist police.

1875-82. Period of Narodnik terrorism influenced by Tkachev and Nechayev's theories of a conspiratorial party.

1879. Zemlya i Volya party splits into factions: terrorist (**Narodnaya Volya**) and agitator (**Chorny Peredel**) led by Plekhanov. **Birth of Trotsky and Stalin.**

1881. Tsar Alexander II assassinated by **Narodovoltsi.**

1883. Formation in Switzerland by former **Chorny Peredel**-ists of first Russian Social-Democratic Marxist group.

1887. Execution of Lenin's elder brother Alexander and fellow **Narodovoltsi** conspirators.

1889. Founding congress in Paris of the **Second Socialist International.** Plekhanov represents Russian Marxist Social-Democracy.

1891-93. Famine, revival of Narodnik populism, mass strikes and massacres of workers. Lenin's first Marxist criticism of Narodism.

1894. Tsarist censorship allows 'Legal' Marxism. Lenin's public activity begins.

1895. Tsar Nicholas II begins his reign with massacre of strikers at Yaroslavl. Lenin's activity as factory organizer cut short by arrest and exile to Siberia till 1900.

1898. Abortive first congress of Russian Social-Democratic Labour Party (RSDLP) in Minsk.

1899. Lenin in exile attacks Social-Democratic **reformism.**

1900. Foundation of newspaper **Iskra** by Lenin, Plekhanov and others in Geneva. Lenin directs the spread of underground party network in Russia.

1901. Veteran Narodniks, Gots, Chernov and others, form **Socialist-Revolutionary Party** (SR) engaged in terrorism.

1903. Second Congress of the RSDLP in Brussels and London ends with the **Bolshevik-Menshevik** split. Lenin resigns from **Iskra.**

1904. Lenin's new paper **Vperyod.** Reorganization of Bolshevik party in Russia. Russo-Japanese War. Plehve assassinated by an SR. Baku oil-workers strike.

1905. Bloody Sunday, general strike and the **first Russian Revolution.** Formations of workers' Soviets in Petersburg, Moscow, etc. and the liberal bourgeois **Kadet** party. Tsarism regains control but concedes a **Duma** (parliament).

Preface

Lenin, the architect of the October Revolution, lies mouldering in his Red Square mausoleum, the last mummified relic of a Big Idea that went disastrously wrong. It cannot be long now before his remains are swept away to make room for a discotheque or MacDonald's annexe.

Lenin's reputation has gone into irreversible decline, from totemic super-hero of the revolution, revered by several generations of international communists, to being vilified and demonized as the founder of Soviet tyranny, and finally sinking to non-person disregarded by history. Is there any reason why we should take him seriously now? The verdict on his case has been passed by history – he has nothing more to say to us.

Commonsense tells us this cannot be so. Negatively, if for no other reason, Lenin's impact on the 20th century history of Russia and Eastern Europe must surely be worth assessing. How else can we hope to understand the way things stand at present, a world we have inherited, shaped by the prolonged struggle between the ideologies of Communism and the capitalist free market, without a grasp of Lenin's original aims in establishing the world's first socialist state?

One mystery will always haunt Lenin's career, and that is an old, much debated and unresolved question. Was he not misguided in striving to implant Marxist socialism in Russia, a backward, essentially peasant economy, when by all accounts Marx himself had prescribed socialism as the next stage of evolution for industrially advanced states in Western Europe? Indeed, the model of this prescription seemed to be the first mass proletarian Social Democratic Party in Germany, growing steadily in the 1890s and early years of the 20th century, and which took a **political** rather than outrightly revolutionary view of Marx.

Nevertheless, in a moment of optimism or impulsiveness, Karl Marx and Friedrich Engels in their 1882 preface to the **Communist Manifesto**, had proclaimed the "open question" of a Russian revolution, basing themselves on the **obshchina**, "a form of the primeval common ownership of land" which might "pass directly to the higher form of communist ownership". On this slender thread of a semi-mythical "village communalism", they hung weighty hopes of an **international** revolution! "If the Russian Revolution becomes the signal for a proletarian revolution in the West, so that both complement each other, the present Russian common ownership of land may serve as the starting point for a communist development."

Lenin's stormy petrel career from the mid-1890s onwards advances rapidly on two fronts: first, vehemently opposing the Russian utopianism of his predecessors with a theoretically more sophisticated **scientific Marxism**; and second, swimming against the mainstream Social Democratic current of politically **reformist** Marxism, and step-by-step creating an élite strike-force Bolshevik Party for the revolutionary seizure of power in Russia.

Lenin's undoubted avantgarde achievement looks to us today like his biggest mistake, and the very reason we find it so hard to assess him objectively, let alone sympathetically.

Lenin for Beginners is certainly not a "how to" book for budding revolutionaries. Besides, is anything more inconceivable in our postmodern era than a "revolutionary Marxist"? If such a creature existed, however, would he or she gain helpful instruction from Lenin's methods? It is unlikely. Lenin addressed conditions in Russia which were unique and of his time. And yet, even readers who feel decidedly non-revolutionary will get more enlightenment from this book if they try to put themselves into Lenin's shoes, and, at each step of the way, relive for themselves Lenin's historical decisions and actions.

Richard Appignanesi
1994

Russian dates before January 31, 1918 follow the old style (Julian) calendar. Subsequent dates follow the new style (Gregorian) calendar, which took effect in February, 1918.

1906. Duma elections. Fourth RSDLP unity congress in Stockholm. Stolypin dissolves the first Duma in July.

1907. Fifth RSDLP congress. Stolypin arrests Social-Democrat deputies and dissolves the second Duma in June. Third Duma opens in November. Lenin leaves Russia — till 1917.

1908-10. The 'Duma Question' causes more factional splits within the RSDLP. Lenin's struggle against Bolshevik anti-Duma fraction.

1912. Prague conference of the Bolshevik party decides to take part in the fourth Duma elections. Legal party paper **Pravda** organized. Massacre of striking workers at Lena Gold Mines.

1914. Outbreak of the First World War. Collapse of the Second International into national 'defensists', pacificists and international 'defeatists'.

1915. Lenin's strategy of **revolutionary defeatism** rejected by first anti-war Zimmerwald conference.

1916. Lenin's position gains support on the International Left. Strikes in Russia increase. Rasputin murdered.

1917. The February Revolution: the Tsar is overthrown. Dual Power 'shared' between Petrograd Soviet and the bourgeois Provisional Government.

February — October: Menshevik and SR leaders of the Soviet support the Provisional government and accept ministerial posts.

April: Lenin returns to Russia. Struggle against Dual Power begins.

May: Kerensky, an ex-SR, heads Provisional Government.

June: Kerensky pursues war against Germany.

July: popular pro-Soviet uprising fails. Counter-revolutionary measures by SR, Menshevik and Provisional Government leadership. Bolshevik party persecuted. Lenin in hiding.

August: Kerensky toys with military dictatorship.

September: Bolsheviks gain majorities in Petrograd and Moscow Soviets.

The October revolution: Lenin leads Bolsheviks to power. Provisional Government put under arrest. Bolsheviks organize Soviet government.

December: peace negotiations with Germany at Brest-Litovsk.

1918. January: Third Congress of Soviets approves dispersal of Constituent Assembly. Germans help form counter-revolutionary 'White' forces in Ukraine. Factory Councils approve Bolshevik party's central management of the economy.

February: Germans occupy key territories and threaten Petrograd.

March: approval of Brest-Litovsk Peace Treaty despite strong Left Communist opposition.

1918-1920. Civil War: struggle against White and Allied forces. War Communism.

1919. Third Communist International founded. General defeat of revolutions outside Russia.

1920-21. Famine, anti-Bolshevik agitation, strikes and peasant unrest. Inner-Party debates led by Left Communists on trade unions, worker-management, expropriation, etc.

1921. March: Kronstadt uprising. At the Tenth Party Congress Lenin launches the **New Economic Policy**, a limited free market and an end to War Communism.

1922. Genoa and Rapallo conferences establish trade with non-Communist countries. Lenin's first stroke — regular work ceases. Lenin's 'last struggle' against bureaucratism and chauvinism, calls for cultural revolution, foresees dangers of Stalinist authoritarianism.

1924. Lenin dies.

LENIN HAS ADVANCED MARXIST THEORY AS A **PRACTICAL FORCE** INTO THE 20th. CENTURY.

Georg Lukacs
(1885-1971)
Hungarian Marxist philosopher and critic

LENIN... THE DREAMER IN THE KREMLIN.

H.G.Wells
Popular historian and science-fiction writer

9

LENIN'S 'GREAT QUESTION

A REVOLUTIONARY PARTY AS THE **ORGANIZED** EXPRESSION OF COLLECTIVE ACTION... THAT WAS LENIN'S STRATEGY AND THE ESSENCE OF **POLITICAL** MARXISM.

Antonio Gramsci (1891-1937) Marxist philosopher, a founder of the Italian Communist Party and organizer of factory soviets in Turin 1919-21.

NOT ONE MAN BUT MILLIONS OF PEOPLE **MADE** THE RUSSIAN REVOLUTION. LENIN REMAINS THE GREATEST MARXIST **TACTICIAN** BECAUSE HE UNDERSTOOD THIS.

In 1894, when Lenin was only 24, the revolution seemed pretty remote. Was Lenin a dreamer or a practical Marxist when he asked . . .

... how must actions aimed at bringing about the socialist system attract the masses in order to yield serious **RESULTS?**

... the answer to this question depends directly and immediately on the way in which the grouping of **social forces** in Russia and the **class struggle** which forms the substance of Russian reality are understood.

THE TSAR'S 'WEDDING-CAKE'

WE RULE YOU

WE FOOL YOU

WE SHOOT YOU

WE EAT FOR YOU

WE FEED ALL

The Tsar's 'wedding-cake' is a cartoon depicting social injustice circa 1890. But the Russian class struggle, as Lenin understood it through Marx, was a lot more complex.

11

TSARISM IS FEUDALISM

THE **STATE** IS IDENTIFIED WITH RUSSIA'S **ABSOLUTE ALL POWERFUL** MONARCH, **THE TSAR** ...
(OR CZAR-IT MEANS 'CAESAR')

TSAR NICHOLAS II (1868-1918)

But where does the "absolute power" of the Tsar come from? Since 1613, the Romanov Tsars depend on the power of the feudal system, i.e., a small noble class which owns both the **land** and **peasant-serfs*** ... (*serf, Latin **servus**=slave)

...LANDLORDS COUNT THEIR WEALTH IN THE NUMBER OF 'SOULS' THEY OWN!

Who administers the State?

The territory of the Tsarist Empire was HUGE, containing peoples of many different races and languages (or 1/10 of the human race by 1870!)

The 'modernizing' Tsar, Peter the Great, in 1722 set up a career-ladder in the civil service (with 14 rungs corresponding to noble and military ranks). Chinovnik: in Russian chin means 'rank' or 'rung of a ladder'. Chinovniki were bureaucrats: life-time servants of the state.

...THAT'S WHY I'M SETTING UP MY **CHINOVNIK** SYSTEM!

...AND SOME ROSE FROM POVERTY TO JOIN THE RANKS OF THE HEREDITARY NOBILITY

YES... BUT ONLY **SOME!** ...AND WHAT'S MORE, THE SYSTEM CREATED AN EDUCATED CLASS OF 'CLIMBERS' **TOTALLY CUT OFF** FROM THE MASS OF THE PEOPLE!

13

Vast peasant uprisings did occur: famous ones, led by Stenka Razin in the 17th century . . .
and Emelyan Pugachev in 1773.

WHICH ENDED BADLY!

On 26th Dec. 1825, army officers inspired by the Jacobin ideals of the French revolution
tried to overthrow Tsar Nicholas I. The Decembrist revolt lasted one day!

The Decembrists were not the last upper-class mavericks who asked the great question of the
19th Century . . .

HOW DO WE RE-JOIN THE PEOPLE?

ATHEIST!

COUNT LEO TOLSTOY (1828-1910) THE GREAT NOVELIST PREACHED NON-VIOLENT POPULISM... BUT OTHERS WERE A LOT MORE REVOLUTIONARY!

The 1861 Reform

Russia's defeat in the Crimean War (1853-56) led to **famine** and **unrest** in the countryside. Tsarism faces its own **big question**: how can the Tsar keep the loyalty of his million-strong army which is 90% serf?

BY A CLEVER MOVE... THE TSAR ABOLISHES SERFDOM IN 1861!

THE **SAME** YEAR THAT CIVIL WAR BROKE OUT BETWEEN THE **DIS**-UNITED STATES OF AMERICA!

THE **U.S.** CIVIL WAR DIDN'T REALLY 'FREE' BLACK PEOPLE

AND THE TSAR'S EMANCIPATION DECREE HASN'T IMPROVED THINGS FOR US EITHER!

The peasants are 'free' but saddled with **redemption payments** (mortgages and taxes) because the Tsar has to **compensate** the ex-serf-owners (who keep most of the land anyway!) The peasants blame the landlords and officials who collect the taxes, not the Tsar, **rodnoi otets** ('our little father') who set them free.

WHAT'S BEHIND THE 1861 REFORM?

After 1861 capitalism developed in Russia so rapidly that **in a few decades** it brought about a transformation which had taken centuries in some of the old countries of Europe.

Lenin

FREEDOM IS GOOD FOR BUSINESS!

BY 1876 THE EXPORT SALE OF GRAIN RISES BY 140%...THE BIG LANDOWNERS ARE MAKING A KILLING!

POPULATION IN 1897

NOBLES - 2 MILLION

MERCHANTS & PROFESSIONALS 700 THOUSAND

CLERGY - 350 THOUSAND

...ONLY OUR NUMBER INCREASES!

PEASANTS - 100 MILLION

URBAN PROLETARIAT 14 MILLION

70% of ex-serfs don't own enough land to feed their families. This landless 'army of the unfed' provides a source of cheap labour for capitalist industry.

...The rapid development of capitalism...

The mixture of capitalist enterprise, feudalism and aristocratic privilege was strange and contradictory. It produced typical 'chinovnik' capitalists like Count S.Y.Witte (1849-1915) who began as a railway manager, rose to Minister of Finance and Economy, gained the title of 'Count.' He put Russia on the Gold Standard, set up banks, foreign loans, etc.

Historians tell us how well capitalism was doing under Tsarism. But they forget to mention that Western shareholders owned 90% of Russia's mines, 50% of her chemical industry, over 40% of her engineering plants, and 42% of her banking stock. Tsarist Russia was virtually a colony!

THE NARODNIKS...

The Narodniks were Russia's first revolutionary socialists. The name comes from narod, 'the people', i.e. the peasants. Narodniks were radical intellectuals (also known as the Intelligentsia) who opted out of the noble and educated classes.

THE PEASANT IS A **NATURAL** SOCIALIST...

ONLY THE PEASANTS' AXES—AND THEIR COMMUNAL ECONOMY—CAN SAVE RUSSIA!

ALEXANDER HERZEN ((1812-70) NOBLE LANDOWNER, PUBLICIST, IN EXILE FROM 1847

N.G. CHERNYSHEVSKY (1828-89) SON OF AN ORTHODOX PRIEST, WRITER, CRITIC AND ECONOMIST ADMIRED BY MARX, IMPRISONED IN SIBERIA 1862-83

KOLOKOL

WHAT IS TO BE DONE?

'THE BELL' HERZEN'S LONDON JOURNAL

A NARODNIK NOVEL

WHAT DO THEY BELIEVE?

that the Tsar's emancipation decree is a fraud
that the peasants are a revolutionary class
that the ancient peasant commune (obshchina)
can serve as the basis for a uniquely Russian peasant socialism
that capitalism is an evil which Russia can avoid by going directly into socialism through a peasant revolution

'Going to the people'

The first Narodnik underground movement, 1862, Zemlya i Volya (zemlya, 'land' and volya, 'will' or 'freedom') was split between the followers of Bakunin and Lavrov.

THE PEASANTS ARE A REVOLUTIONARY FORCE **READY** TO DESTROY THE STATE AND REPLACE IT WITH ANARCHIST COLLECTIVES...

No! FIRST WE MUST **PROPAGATE** SOCIALIST IDEAS AMONG THE PEOPLE AND **EDUCATE** A SUFFICIENT NUMBER OF LEADERS...

MIKHAIL BAKUNIN (1814-76) EX-ARMY OFFICER, NOBLE, INTERNATIONAL REVOLUTIONARY, IMPRISONED 1851-61

P.L. LAVROV (1823-1901) EX-ARMY COLONEL, FRIEND AND TRANSLATOR OF MARX IN EXILE FROM 1870.

Vperyod

'FORWARD' UNDERGROUND POPULIST PAPER

The Narodnik leaders inspired the khozdeniye v narod, "going to the people", movement. In the 'mad summer' of 1874 thousands of well-off young people abandon their university studies to join the people in the countryside. 1874 ends with mass arrests — and the discovery that the peasant masses remain loyal to the Tsar. Naive? Utopian? Yes, but history had never before seen such a mass exodus of intellectuals to the people!

19

The theory of narodnik terrorism

1874 teaches the 'Lavrists' the need for a **disciplined party** ... as outlined by two other Narodnik leaders:

Tkachev's 1874 letter to Lavrov's **Vperyod** predicted that 'Going to the People' would fail.

P.N. Tkachev (1844-85) a nobleman and underground revolutionary. In exile, 1,873, publishes a journal, **Nabat**, (The Tocsin) which advocates the seizure of power by a revolutionary minority in order to implement **socialist reforms** through the machinery of the state.

S.G. Nechayev (1847-82) a school-teacher of working class origins and terrorist who died in prison. With Bakunin he wrote **The Revolutionary Catechism**.

In 1878 Vera Zasulich (1851-1919) shot and wounded Governor Trepov of St. Petersburg who ordered the flogging of a Narodnik student. The court acquitted her, and friends smuggled her abroad before the police could arrest her again.

The Narodniks' political aims were not extreme — land for the people, unions, a parliament, a republic. But they turned to terrorism as the only weapon they had to achieve even the most basic **democratic reforms.**

At a secret party congress in 1879, the question of tactics splits **Zemlya i Volya** into two factions. The **Narodnaya Volya** (people's Freedom or Will) applies terrorism against government officials and even the Tsar.

The assassination of Tsar Alexander II, 1881.

POLICE REPRESSION AND CENSORSHIP PREVENT US FROM **REACHING** THE PEOPLE...

WE MUST **FORCE** THE TSAR TO SURRENDER **POLITICAL LIBERTIES** TO THE PEOPLE!

WE AREN'T BLOODTHIRSTY... BUT TSARISM OFFERS US NO OTHER CHOICE!

Sofia Perovskaya (1853-81) daughter of a Tsarist general began as a teacher in a workers' study group. **A.I. Zhelyabov** (1850-81) came from an ex-serf family. **S.N. Khalturin** (1856-82) a carpenter and founder of the **Northern Union of Russian Workers** who turned to terrorism when this union failed. By 1884, arrests, exile and executions destroyed the small number of **Narodovoltsi** terrorists.

The other Zemlya i Volya faction is **Chorny Peredel**, 'Black Partition', meaning equal land distribution for the 'Black Folk', i.e. the peasants. Its leaders, the ex-mining student Plekhanov and Axelrod, reject terrorism as a weapon of political reform.

WE WERE THE **FIRST** TO UNDERSTAND...

...THAT NARODNIK 'PEASANT SOCIALISM' WAS **UTOPIAN**...

...AND THAT THE **INDUSTRIAL** WORKERS MUST ACT AS RUSSIA'S REVOLUTIONARY **CLASS!**

ZASULICH

P.B. Axelrod (1850-1928) later became a leading Marxist theorist.

George Plekhanov (1856-1918) became known as "the father of Russian Marxism".

In 1883 this exiled trio founded the first Marxist **Emancipation of Labour** group in Switzerland. But what did **Marx** and **Engels** think of Russia?

Marx and Engels were in touch with **three generations** of Russian revolutionaries. Bakunin's translation of the **Communist Manifesto** was printed by Herzen's **Kolokol.** Narodniks like Chernyshevsky impressed Marx and he (and Engels) learned Russian. Marx even wanted to re-write **Das Kapital** to include a section on Russian economy.

But relations with the Russian exiles weren't always smooth!

MARX EXPELS BAKUNIN FROM THE *1*st SOCIALIST INTERNATIONAL IN 1872.

In 1882 Marx and Engels added a preface to Plekhanov's new translation of the **Communist Manifesto**:

"If the Russian Revolution becomes the signal for a proletarian revolution in the West, so that both complement each other, the present Russian common ownership of land (obshchina) may serve as the starting point for a communist development."

But after Marx's death (1883), Engels became impatient with Narodniks' peasant socialism.

WHAT DID ENGELS **MEAN?**

1st 'the people' isn't like yeast which will rise in a single mass . . .
2nd they thought they could 'skip over' capitalism — but capitalism was already there!

Every major revolution in western history (till 1917) has been bourgeois . . .
the English (1642-49), American (1776), French (1789), and German (1849) . . .

THAT'S TRUE. BUT CAPITALISM **SWEEPS AWAY** FEUDALISM, AND BOURGEOIS **DEMOCRATIC** STRUGGLE ACTUALLY BENEFITS THE PROLETARIAT...

a bourgeois revolution always limits itself to democratic transformations which are of advantage to the bourgeoisie itself.

THAT'S WHY THE PROLETARIAT NEEDS A PARTY AS TOUGH AS THE **NARODOVOLTSI**... TO **PUSH** THE BOURGEOIS REVOLUTION FURTHER THAN IT LIKES TO GO!

And according to Engels the 1849 bourgeois revolution in Germany might have succeeded...

...IF THE REAL MUSCLE HAD COME FROM PEASANTS AND WORKERS!

...A SHORT BIOGRAPHY...

LENIN... WAS BORN **VLADIMIR ILYICH ULYANOV,** APRIL 10, 1870 AT **SIMBIRSK** (TODAY ULYANOVSK) A PROVINCIAL CAPITAL ON THE VOLGA

LENIN'S MOTHER: **MARIA ALEXANDROVNA BLANK** THE DAUGHTER OF A SURGEON AND LANDOWNER. SHE DIED IN 1916.

HIS FATHER; **ILYA NIKOLAEYICH ULYANOV** WAS... **A CHINOVNIK:** AN INSPECTOR OF PUBLIC SCHOOLS PROMOTED TO THE NOBLE RANK OF 'CIVIL COUNCILLOR' IN 1874...

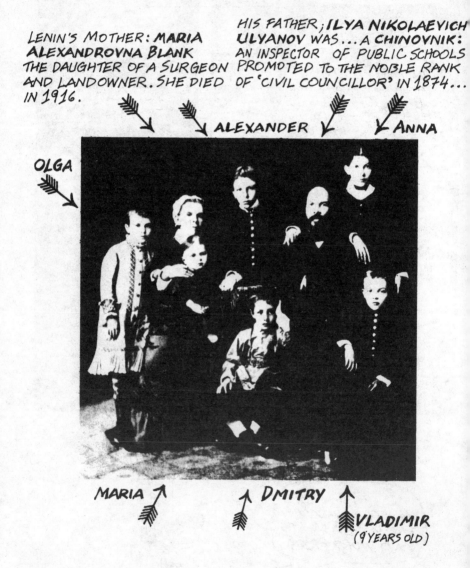

OLGA

ALEXANDER

ANNA

MARIA

DMITRY

VLADIMIR (9 YEARS OLD)

"By their social status, the founders of
modern scientific socialism, Marx and Engels,
themselves belonged to the bourgeois
intelligentsia."

Lenin

LENIN INHERITED HIS FATHER'S
TARTAR EYES, HIGH CHEEKBONES
RED HAIR (AND BALDNESS)...
LIKE HIS FATHER, HE ALSO
DIED OF BRAIN HEMORRHAGE.

LENIN'S BROTHER ALEXANDER,
BORN 1866 (NICKNAMED
'SASHA')

FROM ME, HE
'INHERITED' SOMETHING
ELSE...

29

Sasha... The Revolutionary

VERY SERIOUS, INTELLIGENT, QUIET... HE SEEMED A MODEL STUDENT AT ST. PETERSBURG UNIVERSITY...
IN 1886 – THE YEAR OF HIS FATHER'S DEATH, – SASHA WON A GOLD MEDAL FOR HIS ZOOLOGICAL STUDY OF ANNELID WORMS...
SOME MONTHS LATER HE PAWNED IT TO BUY DYNAMITE

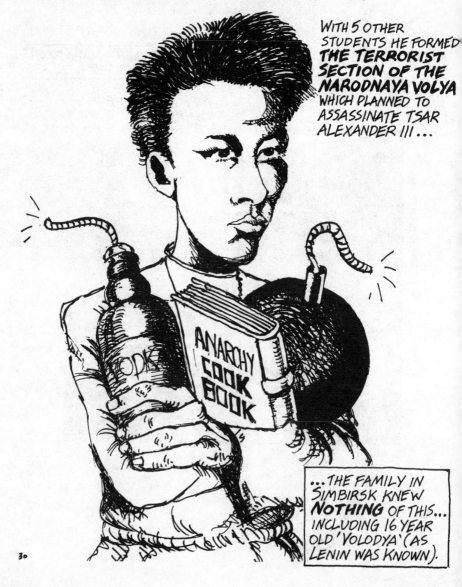

WITH 5 OTHER STUDENTS HE FORMED **THE TERRORIST SECTION OF THE NARODNAYA VOLYA** WHICH PLANNED TO ASSASSINATE TSAR ALEXANDER III...

...THE FAMILY IN SIMBIRSK KNEW **NOTHING** OF THIS... INCLUDING 16 YEAR OLD 'VOLODYA' (AS LENIN WAS KNOWN).

By accident, the Pertersburg police discovered the plot. Sasha was arrested, tried . . . and on May 8, 1887 he and four comrades were hanged . . .

At his trial Sasha declared: "we are encouraged to develop our intellectual powers, but we are not allowed to use them for the benefit of the people."

...A TYPICAL NARODNIK?

PARTLY... BUT HE TRIED TO COMBINE NARODNIK BELIEFS WITH SCIENTIFIC MARXISM...

Just before his arrest Sasha had translated Marx's **Critique of Hegel's Philosophy of Right** (1844). Lenin's sister, Anna (arrested with Sasha in 1887, but later released and banished from Petersburg) reports that: "When Volodya heard this, he immediately sat down and read it!"

IN AUGUST 1887, LENIN ENTERS **KAZAN** UNIVERSITY TO STUDY LAW...

THANKS TO THE WARM RECOMMEDATION OF MY FORMER HEADMASTER, **FEODOR KERENSKY**,* A DECENT FELLOW...

* A NAME WE'LL SEE AGAIN IN 1917!

BUT VOLODYA WAS SOON MIXED UP IN A STUDENT DEMONSTRATION, ARRESTED, AND EXPELLED FROM THE UNIVERSITY, DEC 5, 1887!

YOU'RE UP AGAINST A STONE WALL, YOUNG MAN!

YES, A **ROTTEN** ONE WHICH'LL COLLAPSE AT A KICK!

Banished from Kazan, Lenin is permitted to join his sister Anna at their mother's estate in Kukushkino, 30 miles away. Both are now under police supervision ... and Maria Alexandrovna arrives with the younger children to look after these two dangerous 'criminals' ...

Lenin studies hard at this time — but he keeps fit! Lenin was a fine swimmer, fancy skater, enjoyed mountain-climbing and hunting.

In the autumn of '88, he is allowed to re-enter Kazan but not the university ... the police consider him "an undesirable"

LENIN FREQUENTS
A MARXIST GROUP
LED BY **N.E.**
FEDOSEYEV
(1871·98)

...AND ALMOST GET
MYSELF ARRESTED
AGAIN!

July '89 the police round up the Kazan group. Fedoseyev later commits suicide in Siberia.

LENIN TURNS TO THE WRITINGS OF THE EXILED 'FATHER OF RUSSIAN MARXISM'...

'THE NARODNAYA VOLYA MUST BECOME A MARXIST PARTY... OR REMAIN STAGNANT'

PLEKHANOV'S FIRST MARXIST TREATISE HAD THE **SAME** IMPACT AS THE **COMMUNIST MANIFESTO** BACK IN 1848!

G.V. PLEKHANOV
SOCIALISM
AND THE
POLITICAL
STRUGGLE
1883

October 1889: the Ulyanov family moves to Samara, a 'backwater' Volga town without industry or university. But many old **Narodovoltsi** released from Siberia live there under police surveillance.

VOLODYA PUMPS THE VETERANS FOR INFORMATION ON **UNDERGROUND METHODS...**

Finally in 1890 the authorities permit him to take his exams in Petersburg as an 'external' student (which means in 'quarantine'). He runs through a 4 year law course in less than a year and comes out first, 27 Nov. 1891, and still has time to translate the **Communist Manifesto**!

LENIN WORKS FOR A TIME AS A JUNIOR ATTORNEY IN SAMARA...
BUT NOT FOR LONG...

The first-ever translation of Marx's **Das Kapital** appears in Russian by the Narodnik economist N.F. Danielson in 1872.

NARODNIKS KNEW ABOUT MARX'S IDEAS - BUT MISUNDERSTOOD THEM OR USED THEM UNSCIENTIFICALLY.

PLEKHANOV

CAPITALISM IS AN EVIL WHICH RUSSIA CAN WELL DO WITHOUT!

N.K. MIKHAILOVSKY (1842-1902)
a popular Narodnik veteran attacks Marxism on moral and economic grounds in his journal, Russkoe Bogatstvo (Russia's Wealth) in 1874.

BUT THE TSARIST POLICE, TOO, ARE INTERESTED IN MARXISM!

Like the Narodniks, the police believe capitalism (or Marx's criticism of it) has **no relevance** to Russia. Narodism is the only real danger they see!

IT'S JUST A THEORY, QUITE HARMLESS...

WHO'S GOING TO UNDERSTAND IT ANYWAY?

CAPITAL KARL MARX

SINCE THE MARXISTS OPPOSE NARODISM - LET'S ENCOURAGE THEM!

1894: THE ORIGIN OF 'LEGAL MARXISM'

IN 1894, THE CENSOR ALLOWS THE PUBLICATION BY A RUSSIAN MARXIST WHICH CRITICIZES NARODISM...

...THE BEGINNING OF 'LEGAL MARXISM'

In the next 5 years, Tsarist censorship approves Marxist texts which it hopes are too heavy and obscure for the public . . .

BIG MISTAKE! OUR BOOKS ARE **DEVOURED** BY THE YOUNG...

CRITICAL NOTES ON THE PROBLEMS OF THE ECONOMIC DEVELOPMENT OF RUSSIA

P.B. STRUVE (1870-1944)

ON THE QUESTION OF THE DEVELOPMENT OF THE MONISTIC VIEW OF HISTORY

PLEKHANOV'S STUDY OF MARXIST MATERIALISM

But in a Marxist circle, St. Petersburg 1894, Lenin expresses strong doubts about Struve's 'new brand' of Marxism.

...A STRANGE FORM OF MARXISM IS BECOMING FASHIONABLE...

LENIN'S INTUITION ABOUT 'REFORMISM'

Sturve's **liberalism** turned him against Marxism — and he ended up a Monarchist supporting the military suppression of socialism in 1917!

Lenin's closest comrade...

LENIN WAS ALREADY KNOWN IN ST. PETERSBURG BEFORE HE ARRIVED HERE IN 1893...

... HIS WORK, CAREFULLY HAND-WRITTEN, HAD BEEN PASSED ROUND AMONG OUR COMRADES ...

NADEZHDA KONSTANTINOVNA KRUPSKAYA (1869-1939)

In her **Memoirs**, Lenin's wife-to-be describes their first encounter at a small gathering of Marxists in the spring of '94.

"Vladimir Ilyich spoke little and was more occupied in contemplating those present. People who styled themselves Marxists became uncomfortable beneath his fixed gaze ... Someone was saying – I think it was Shevlyagin – that it was very important to work in the Committee for Illiteracy. Vladimir Ilyich laughed ... "Well," he said, "if anyone wants to save the fatherland in the Committee for Illiteracy, we won't stop him.""

... A DRY, IRONICAL, VERY RUSSIAN LAUGH...

THE MASSES NEED SOMETHING **MORE** THAN SPOONFULS OF ALPHABET SOUP...

WHO IS KRUPSKAYA?

She came from an impoverished upper class family. Her father had been suspended from the civil service for 'liberalism'. At 14 she began earning her living by teaching. In 1894 she joined the first Petersburg Marxist circle and taught at working men's evening and 'Sunday' schools.

After the 1917 Revolution she was Commissar for Adult Education. Krupskaya was always a fighter for Lenin's ideas.

THAT NIGHT, LENIN WALKS HER HOME AND...

43

WHAT FACTS?

SINCE 1861, CAPITALIST PRODUCTION HAS TRANSFORMED THE **CLASS NATURE** OF THE PEASANTS...

THEY ARE NOT A SINGLE **FEUDAL** MASS ANYMORE...

15% BECOME RICH LANDOWNERS
THE RURAL BOURGEOISIE
(OR A **KULAK**="FIST" IN RUSSIAN)

65% HAVE LITTLE OR NO LAND
THE RURAL PROLETARIAT

20% ARE SMALL LANDHOLDERS
THE RURAL PETTY BOURGEOISIE

"The peasants are not united by working in big enterprises; on the contrary, they are disunited by their small, individual farming. Unlike the workers, they do not see before them an open, obvious, single enemy in the person of the capitalist. They are themselves to a certain extent masters and proprietors."

THE 'TWO SOULS' OF THE PEASANT:

THE PROLETARIAN SAYS TO THE SMALL PEASANT:

YOU ARE SEMI-PROLETARIAN, SO **FOLLOW THE LEAD** OF THE WORKERS; IT IS YOUR ONLY SALVATION.

THE BOURGEOIS SAYS TO THE SMALL PEASANT:

YOU ARE A SMALL PROPRIETOR A **LABOURING FARMER** LABOUR ECONOMY 'GROWS' UNDER CAPITALISM AS WELL. YOU SHOULD BE WITH THE PROPRIETORS, NOT WITH THE PROLETARIAT.

THE SMALL PROPRIETOR HAS **TWO SOULS**: ONE IS A PROLETARIAN AND THE OTHER A 'PROPRIETORY' SOUL.

BUT LOOK AT THE URBAN WORKERS THEY OWN NOTHING BUT THEIR LABOUR POWER...

"The very conditions of their lives make the workers capable of struggle and impel them to struggle. Capital collects the workers in great masses in big cities, uniting them, teaching them to act in unison. At every step the workers come face to face with their main enemy – the capitalist class. In combat with this enemy the worker becomes a **socialist**, comes to realise the necessity of a complete reconstruction of the whole of society, the complete abolition of all poverty and oppression."

45

LENIN BECOMES A FACTORY AGITATOR

emember for example, how the material about the Thornton factory was collected. It was
cided that I should send for a pupil of mine named Krolikov, a sorter in that factory, who had
eviously been deported from Petersburg. I was to collect from him all information according to
plan drawn up by Vladimir Ilyich. Krolikov arrived in a fine fur coat he had borrowed from
meone and brought a whole exercise-book full of information, which he further supplemented
rbally. This data was very valuable. In fact Vladimir Illyich fairly pounced on it. Afterwards I
d Apollinaria Alexandrovna Yakubova put kerchiefs on our heads and made ourselves look like
omen factory-workers, and went personally to the Thornton factory-barracks, visiting both the
ngle and married quarter. Conditions were most appalling. It was solely on the basis of material
thered in this manner that Vladimir Ilyich wrote his letters and leaflets. Examine his leaflets
ddressed to the working men and women of the Thornton factory. The detailed knowledge of
e subject they deal with is at once apparent. And what a schooling this was for all the comrades
orking then!

KRUPSKAYA, 'MEMORIES OF LENIN'.

47

Lenin meets other Marxists working in Vilna, Moscow and Kiev. He is soon known as the **Starik** (the 'old man') and in 1895, with Martov, he founds the . . .

'LEAGUE OF STRUGGLE FOR THE EMANCIPATION OF THE WORKING CLASS'

MARTOV
(Julius Tsederbaum) 1873-1923
has first-hand experience of strike-action
among Jewish socialist workers (the **Bund**).
The first mass strike of 15,000 Bundists
occurs at a Bialystok textile industry in 1895.

NOTE: AT THIS TIME, MARXISTS CALLED THEMSELVES **SOCIAL-DEMOCRATS**

WHAT IS SOCIAL-DEMOCRACY?

THE BRITISH LABOUR PARTY? SWEDEN? WILLY BRANDT?

NOT EXACTLY... IT STARTED IN THE 1860's AS A COMPLICATED ATTEMPT TO UNITE THE SOCIALIST FACTIONS IN GERMANY...

Ferdinand Lassalle (1825-64), Marx's rival in Germany, borrowed the name social-democracy from French republicanism of the 1840s.

In 1875, at Gotha, Lassalle's faction and the 'Eisenachers' led by the Marxist Wilhelm Liebknecht united to form the German Social-Democratic Party.

Marx wasn't completely happy!

Bismarck (1815-98) the Prussian 'Iron Chancellor' who united Germany.

Despite Bismarck's attempts to outlaw it, the SDP became the fastest-growing workers' party in the world, gaining many seats in the German parliament.

Social-Democratic Marxism was defined by Engels and Karl Kautsky in the Erfurt Programme of 1891. Socialists everywhere

looked up to the SDP as the great, successful 'model' . . .

Paris, 1889: at the founding congress of the **Second Socialist International** (the First, 1864-76, was led by Marx) Plekhanov is the spokesman for Russian Social-Democracy.

THE RUSSIAN REVOLUTION WILL TRIUMPH AS THE REVOLUTION OF THE **WORKING CLASS**... OR ELSE NOT AT ALL!

...THE INTERNATIONAL IN THE 90'S INCLUDED SOCIALISTS OF VERY DIFFERENT 'TENDENCIES'

JEAN JAURES
SYLVIA PANKHURST
KEIR HARDIE
OTTO BAUER
ROSA LUXEMBURG
KARL LIEBKNECHT
AUGUST BEBEL
DANIEL DELEON

In the spring of '95, Lenin suffering from nervous exhaustion, travels round Europe for 4 months . . . he meets Plekhanov and Axelrod in Switzerland, Kautsky in Germany and in Paris:

CAN YOU RUSSIANS **UNDERSTAND** MARX, WHEN WE IN EUROPE HAVE FORGOTTEN **HOW** ?

PAUL LAFARGUE
(1842-1911) MARX'S SON-IN-LAW

BACK AGAIN IN ST. PETERSBURG, LENIN STEPS UP **STRIKE AGITATION** IN THE FACTORIES. BUT THE POLICE CLOSE IN AND LENIN IS ARRESTED, DEC. 1895

From his cell #193 Lenin continues to direct strike activities . . .

...WRITING MESSAGES IN MILK FROM INKSTANDS OF BLACK BREAD...

In May, 1896, Lenin's **League** militates in a mass strike of 30,000 workers. 20 factories across Russia are affected!

Krupskaya is arrested 8 months after Lenin. Without trial, Lenin is sentenced to 3 years exile in Siberia, 25 Feb. 1897.

51

LENIN ENDS UP IN SHUSHENSKOE, A VILLAGE IN YENISSEI PROVINCE, KNOWN AS THE 'SIBERIAN RIVIERA' (BEING THE SON OF A NOBLE OFFICIAL HAS **SOME** ADVANTAGES !)
KRUPSKAYA IS PERMITTED TO JOIN HIM ON CONDITION THAT THEY MARRY LEGALLY. SHE ARRIVES MAY 1898, ACCOMPANIED BY HER MOTHER ...

POOR MARTOV ISN'T SO LUCKY... UP THERE IN THE ARCTIC CIRCLE !

The Tsarist deep-freeze

...ILLNESS, MADNESS, **SUICIDE AND DEPRESSION** ARE WORSE THAN THE COLD. SHUSHENSKOE HAS ONLY 2 OTHER EXILES... BUT LENIN PREFERS IT THAT WAY...

...EXILES BUNCHED TOGETHER BECOME NEUROTIC!

PREPARE FOR THE COMING STRUGGLE

He exercises, gives the peasants free legal advice ... and since he can have books mailed to him, starts to work like a demon.– With Krupskaya, he translates Vol. 1 of Beatrice and Sidney Webb's **Industrial Democracy**.

He finishes a massive analysis, **The Development of Capitalism in Russia**, published legally (1899) under the name V.Ilyin. For this work, Lenin studied 299 statistical sources in Russian, 38 in German, French and English!

...MEANWHILE, OUTSIDE SIBERIA,

In March '98, at Minsk, a congress calling for a unified national **Russian Social-Democratic Party** ends with most of the delegates arrested.

The real threat to Party unity is internal.
The reformist tendency which Lenin spotted
in Struve's book now becomes an active,
new doctrine known as . . .

ECONOMISM!

LENIN WRITES TO MARTOV

THE 'ECONOMISTS' ACTUALLY ARGUE **AGAINST** AN INDEPENDENT WORKERS PARTY **!**

...AND THEY **DARE** TO CALL THEMSELVES MARXISTS?

WORSE ... THE 'ECONOMISTS' RELY ON THE GREAT PRESTIGE OF A LEADING GERMAN SOCIAL- DEMOCRAT, A FRIEND OF ENGELS **!**

MARX IS GOING OUT OF DATE... CAPITALISM CAN BE **REFORMED** AND GRADUALLY CHANGED INTO SOCIALISM...

EDUARD BERNSTEIN (1850 - 1932)

THIS BRAND OF PSEUDO-MARXISM IS KNOWN AS **REVISIONISM.**

LENIN FIGHTS BACK

In a hectic 2 weeks Lenin translates Kautsky's attack on Bernstein and writes his own reply, **Protest by Russian Social-Democrats,** August 1899. "If the economic struggle is taken as something complete in itself," Lenin wrote, "there will be **nothing socialist** in it. . ." Lenin's reply united many confused Social-Democrats all over Russia.

Lenin is released, Feb. 1900, and forms a **troika** (alliance) with 2 other exiles, Martov and Potresov. Krupskaya is stuck with another year of exile in Ufa, a town in the Urals.

Lenin has a plan to start an All-Party underground newspaper, **ISKRA**. Lenin crosses the Russian frontier, July 1900.

ISKRA...

LENIN TAKES THE NAME FROM THE **DECEMBRIST** SLOGAN:

"OUT OF THIS SPARK (**ISKRA**) SHALL SPRING THE FLAME!"

BUT... THE FIRST EDITORIAL MEETING IN GENEVA, AUGUST 1900 NEARLY ENDS IN DISASTER...

THE **SPARK** WAS NEARLY EXTINGUISHED!

A PRETTY POOR START!

TO BREAK THE THE DEADLOCK PLEKHANOV SHOULD HAVE TWO VOTES...

AXELROD   ZASULICH

Plekhanov, the "father of Russian Marxism", disagrees about tactics. He is suspicious (and a little jealous) of the younger generation. During his long exile, he has lost touch with the mass labour movement developing in Russia.

WHAT'S SO IMPORTANT ABOUT A NEWSPAPER?

Lenin remained in control of **Iskra**. He got round Plekhanov's extra vote by setting up in Munich. Lenin was determined to go ahead with an extraordinary plan: **Iskra** must serve to **create** a Party!

ISKRA DISTRIBUTION ≈ PARTY WORK!

E TOUGH UNDERCOVER 'AGENTS' WHO SMUGGLE *ISKRA* INTO
JSSIA ARE PERSONALLY INSTRUCTED BY LENIN TO **ORGANIZE**
ID **COORDINATE** AN **UNDERGROUND PARTY** NETWORK
THE FACTORIES, SOCIAL-DEMOCRATIC LOCAL COMMITTEE
UDY CIRCLES ETC, ETC, ALL OVER RUSSIA...

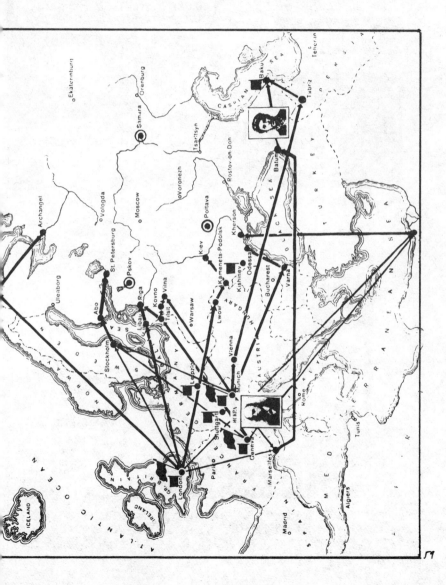

BUT RUSSIA IS BIG, TSARISM IS POWERFUL

The first issue of **Iskra** appears, December 1900, with the secret help of German Social-Democrats. Copies were smuggled into Russia inside shoes, books, toys, ladies corsets, waistcoats etc . . . But the police are alert . . .

> . . . PERHAPS ONLY **ONE-TENTH** OF ANY ISSUE GOT THROUGH!

> BUT EVEN A **SINGLE** COPY COULD BE **REPRODUCED** BY SECRET PRINTING PRESSES AND DISTRIBUTED LOCALLY!

Krupskaya released from exile, works as a one-woman admini-strator of Iskra.

like the famous illegal Baku press in the Caucasus which **re-printed Iskra** by the thousands!

L. B. Krasin (1870-1926) engineer, explosives expert, chief Bolshevik organizer in Russia, sets up an illegal press at Baku.

FOR THE FIRST TIME, A LEADER **IN EXILE** REALLY WORKS TOGETHER WITH **SCATTERED** REVOLUTIONARIES BACK HOME. THAT'S THE IMPORTANCE OF **ISKRA** AS THE "BACKBONE OF MILITANT PARTY ORGANIZATION."

WHAT IS TO BE DONE?

'GIVE US AN ORGANIZATION OF REVOLUTIONARIES, AND WE WILL OVERTURN RUSSIA!'

LENIN SPELLS OUT HIS IDEAS ON PARTY ORGANIZATION IN ISKRA ARTICLES AND IN AN IMPORTANT BOOK: WHAT IS TO BE DONE?, 1902

THE SAME TITLE AS CHERNYSHEVSKY'S FAMOUS NARODNIK NOVEL (WRITTEN IN PRISON, 1863.)

... I maintain (1) that no revolutionary movement can be durable without a stable organization of leaders which preserves continuity; (2) that the broader the mass which is spontaneously drawn into the struggle ... the more urgent is the necessity for such an organization ... because the broader the mass, the easier it is for any demagogue to attract the backward sections of the mass; (3) that such an organization must consist mainly of people who are professionally engaged in revolutionary activities; (4) that, in an autocratic country, the more we narrow the membership of such an organization ... the more difficult will it be to 'catch' such an organization; and (5) the wider will be the category of people, both from the working class and from other classes of society, who will have an opportunity of participating in the movement and actively working in it.

...in WHAT IS TO BE DONE? Lenin argues:

... the working class exclusively by its own efforts is able to develop only trade-union consciousness ... Class political consciousness can be brought to the workers **only from without**, that is, only from outside the economic struggle, from outside the sphere of relations between workers and employers.

BUT BY 1903 **WORKERS** WERE THE **LEADING FORCE** AGAINST TSARISM!

MASS STRIKES ALL ACROSS THE UKRAINE, AND TRANSCAUCASIA, VIOLENT CLASHES WITH THE POLICE AND COSSACK TROOPS, BARRICADES IN MOSCOW

WORKERS THEMSELVES HAVE SMASHED 'PEACEFUL ECONOMISM' INTO PIECES!

DOESN'T LENIN CONTRADICT HIMSELF?

... IN FACT, **WHAT IS TO BE DONE?** IS DIRECTED MAINLY **AGAINST** A CONFUSED AND DIVIDED INTELLIGENTSIA. IT'S TRUE, LENIN SAYS SCIENTIFIC SOCIALISM "CAME OUT OF THE HEADS" OF INTELLECTUALS LIKE MARX AND ENGELS... **BUT...**

OUR INTELLECTUALS DON'T HAVE HEADS LIKE **THAT!**

1 ... an organization of full-time **professional** revolutionaries must **erase** any distinction between workers and intellectuals.

2 I'm not saying the professionals will "think for everyone" ... because professional revolutionaries will come from the **masses** in ever-increasing numbers!

Lenin's strategy

During this period of mass strike activity, the majority of local Social-Democratic committees in Russia are fused into the Iskra network.

Constant visits from escaped prisoners, exiles, and hundreds of letters from workers, keep Lenin well-informed.

A 'young eagle' escaped from Siberia visits Lenin in London: **Lev Davidovich Bronstein**, from a family of Jewish farmers in the Ukraine, union organizer in Odessa, and nicknamed **Pero** ('The Pen'). He is better known today as . . .

TROTSKY (1879·1940)

A MAN OF TALENT — HE WILL GO FAR!

NOTHING DOING! BESIDES, I DON'T LIKE THE WRITINGS OF THIS 'PEN'!...

Lenin wants to place the young 'Pen' on the Iskra board, but Plekhanov won't have it!

Preparations begin in 1902 for an All-Party Congress. **Iskra** calls on leading S—D exiles in Europe, agents and revolutionaries in Russia to establish a **united Party** with a single programme and constitution.

Lenin is the real organizer, working flat out on reports, resolutions, speeches, leaving nothing to chance.

1903: THE 2nd CONGRESS OF THE RUSSIAN SOCIAL DEMOCRATIC LABOUR PARTY

The '2nd' in honour of the abortive 1898 Minsk Congress. Veteran exiles, like Plekhanov and Zasulich, have waited 20 years for this! With tears in their eyes, the delegates sing **THE INTERNATIONAL**.

The first of 37 sessions opens July 17, 1903, in a Brussels warehouse infested with lice and rats. Plagued by spies, harassed by Belgian and Russian police, the Congress moves to London in August.

Iskra's leadership seems guaranteed. Out of 51 votes, Lenin has secured 33 for **Iskra**, thanks to careful preparation.
Iskra's chief rival, the 'economist' paper **Rabochee Dyelo** (Worker's Cause) has only 3.
❝ The Jewish Bund has 5, and 6 remain unaligned . . .

Everything goes well — until the 22nd session. Discussion opens on **definition of Party** **membership**, Paragraph I of the Party Rules.

Lenin was repeating what he had already said in 1902 in his What Is To Be Done? that the Party, as the vanguard of the proletariat, should be as organized as possible.

But Lenin is outvoted 28 to 23. Martov's majority includes Economists and Bundists.

A.S MARTYNOV (1865-1935) 'ECONOMIST' LEADER

A. KREMER A LEADING BUNDIST

The 27th session...

CHECK MATE IN 2 MOVES!

1st move: the Bundists move to remain an autonomous organization of Jewish workers. Defeated by 41 votes, they walk out.

2nd move: Congress decides that **Iskra** is the sole representative of the Party abroad. Now the Economists walk out!

Martov has lost 8 votes!

With his majority, Lenin forms a Central Committee of 3 Iskrists to operate inside Russia. Plekhanov is voted Chairman of the Party Council.

BETTER FEWER, BUT BETTER!

Next comes the election of editors to the **Iskra** board (now the **central organ** of the Party). Everyone expects the re-election of the original six. But Lenin pushes through a new editorship of only 3: Plekhanov, Martov and himself ...

the BOLSHEVIK~MENSHEVIK split...

The **Iskra** debate drags on for 9 bitter sessions, splitting the Party into pro-Lenin Bolsheviks ('majority') and Mensheviks ('minority').

The Congress ends with everyone exhausted, depressed, and only 4 out of 24 items on the agenda decided!

THE SPLIT: SOME **NEGATIVE** ASPECTS

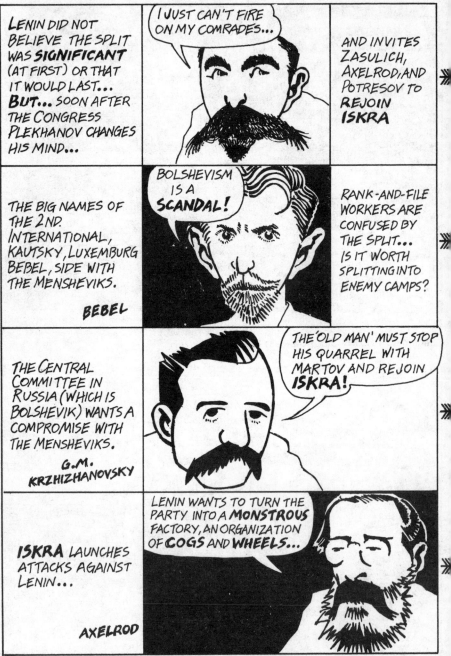

LENIN DID NOT BELIEVE THE SPLIT WAS **SIGNIFICANT** (AT FIRST) OR THAT IT WOULD LAST... **BUT...** SOON AFTER THE CONGRESS PLEKHANOV CHANGES HIS MIND...

I JUST CAN'T FIRE ON MY COMRADES...

AND INVITES ZASULICH, AXELROD, AND POTRESOV TO **REJOIN ISKRA**

THE BIG NAMES OF THE 2ND. INTERNATIONAL, KAUTSKY, LUXEMBURG, BEBEL, SIDE WITH THE MENSHEVIKS.

BEBEL

BOLSHEVISM IS A **SCANDAL!**

RANK-AND-FILE WORKERS ARE CONFUSED BY THE SPLIT... IS IT WORTH SPLITTING INTO ENEMY CAMPS?

THE CENTRAL COMMITTEE IN RUSSIA (WHICH IS BOLSHEVIK) WANTS A COMPROMISE WITH THE MENSHEVIKS.

G.M. KRZHIZHANOVSKY

THE 'OLD MAN' MUST STOP HIS QUARREL WITH MARTOV AND REJOIN **ISKRA!**

ISKRA LAUNCHES ATTACKS AGAINST LENIN...

AXELROD

LENIN WANTS TO TURN THE PARTY INTO A **MONSTROUS** FACTORY, AN ORGANIZATION OF **COGS** AND **WHEELS**...

SOME **POSITIVE** ASPECTS

LENIN RESIGNS IN DISGUST... THE MOST TALENTED WRITERS AND INTELLECTUALS ARE ON THE MENSHEVIK SIDE... BUT LENIN STARTS HIS OWN BOLSHEVIK PAPER, **VPERYOD**, DEC. 1904 WITH...

GORKY BOGDANOV LUNACHARSKY

BIG DIFFERENCES CAN GROW FROM LITTLE ONES...

... AND THE REAL **REVOLUTIONARY DIFFERENCE** BETWEEN MENSHEVISM AND BOLSHEVISM WOULD BE **PROVEN** VERY SOON!

BUT EVEN 'CONCILIATORY' BOLSHEVIK COMMITTEE-MEN ARE FINALLY WON OVER LENIN REBUILDS AN UNDERGROUND BOLSHEVIK NETWORK IN RUSSIA.

L.B.KRASIN
(1870·1926)

L.B.KAMENEV
(1883-1936)

WHAT KIND OF MARXIST USES 'FACTORY' AS AN ACCUSATION?!

... ONLY AN UNDISCIPLINED INTELLECTUAL. WHAT COMES SO HARD TO THE BOURGEOIS INTELLECTUAL – **ORGANIZATION** – IS EASILY ACQUIRED BY THE PROLETARIAT BECAUSE OF THEIR **FACTORY** EXPERIENCE.

MEANWHILE... >>>>>→

War between Russia and Japan...

The Russo-Japanese War, Feb. 1904 — Sept. 1905, was an imperialist scramble for colonies in Manchuria, China and Korea. Britain wants a weak Russia in the Far East and backs Japan. France has imperial ambitions and finances the Tsar.

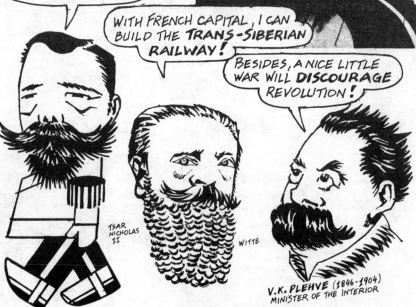

THE FRENCH CONNECTION...

...OVER A **BILLION IN GOLD** RAISED ON THE PARIS STOCK EXCHANGE PAYS FOR THE WAR!

WITH FRENCH CAPITAL, I CAN BUILD THE **TRANS-SIBERIAN RAILWAY!**

BESIDES, A NICE LITTLE WAR WILL **DISCOURAGE** REVOLUTION!

TSAR NICHOLAS II

WITTE

V.K. PLEHVE (1846-1904)
MINISTER OF THE INTERIOR

74

Rural unemployment runs to 10 million. Famines occur in 1895-6, 97 and 1901. Land rent doubles and export of grain goes on at higher profit. The Tsar's "little war" will end in defeat.
Writing in Vperyod, 14 Jan. 1905, Lenin predicts a revolution!

...EVERY STEP BRINGS US NEARER TO A **GREAT NEW WAR**, THE PEOPLE'S WAR AGAINST ABSOLUTISM, THE WAR OF THE PROLETARIAT FOR FREEDOM!

LONG LIVE THE ARMY!

STRUVE, NOW A LEADER OF THE LIBERALS IN EXILE SUPPORTS THE WAR EFFORT...

The elements of bourgeois revolution

Except for the very rich, every sector of society is dissatisfied by 1905. The shortage of **domestic capital** blocks the up-and-coming merchants, Kulaks, industrialists and professionals.

The liberal bourgeoisie organizes a party of **parliamentary opposition** to Tsarism in 1905: the **Constitutional Democrats** (known as 'Kadets' from their initials **kah-deh**)

P.N. Milyukov (1849-1943)
Historian and a Kadet founder.

Narodism revives among the Intelligentsia as the **Socialist-Revolutionary Party** (known as 'SRs') in 1901 . . . a terrorist elite which hopes to lead a single party of workers, peasants and urban petty-bourgeois.

The secret police (**Okhrana**) planted their agents in all revolutionary parties including the Bolshevik. **Yevno Azef**, the SR leader, was an Okhrana agent recruited with Minister Plehve's approval. In July 1904 Plehve was killed in an SR bomb plot engineered by Azef himself!

AR GOTS (SR)

CATHERINE BRESHKO-BRESHKOVSKAYA (SR)

SRs ARE ONLY *LIBERALS ARMED WITH BOMBS!* REFORMISTS AND TERRORISTS ARE TWO SIDES OF THE SAME COIN — NEITHER HAVE ANY FAITH IN THE MASSES!

Colonel S.V. Zubatov (1864-1917), chief of Moscow Security Police, organizes police-controlled trade unions designed to keep out revolutionaries. But the workers used these Zubatov 'unions' to organize strikes in 1902-03. The police have to play along — even paying relief money!

77

POLICE SOCIALISM BACKFIRES

The Zubatov agent, ex-prison chaplain Father **George Gapon** found himself at the head of a big strike, Jan. 9, 1905, started by the Putilov Engineering workers.

Gapon organizes the workers' demands . . .

'Bloody Sunday' Jan 9, 1905

Gapon leads a procession of 200 thousand Petersburg workers to the Tsar's Winter Palace. The troops have orders to fire on the petitioners — and a thousand people are cut down.

Gapon's anger sums up the popular feeling . . .

112 Industrial towns and 10 railway lines declare a **General Strike!** On June 14th the battleship **Potemkin** mutinies and sails under the red flag for 11 days.

TRUST THE WORKERS!

Gapon escapes and arrives in Geneva, spring of 1905. Lenin is only Social-Democrat exile eager to talk to him. Why?

... BECAUSE ANYONE **THAT** CLOSE TO THE **WORKING MASSES** IS WORTH MEETING!

STUDY MARX, LITTLE FATHER OR YOU'LL END UP **DEAD!**

The Bolshevik Central Committee in St. Petersburg warns Lenin that Gapon is "a shady character" (in fact, Gapon was executed by SRs as a police traitor in 1906.)

. . . 'Zubatovism' did socialism a great favour by **legalizing** the working-class movement. By imitating a Social-Democratic movement, Zubatov unwittingly helped to create a **real basis** for it. The striking workers have gone far beyond Gapon, towards an armed uprising of the people! Our Bolshevik Central Committee in Russia failed to see this in time. And so, Menshevik agitators have taken the lead!

BUT WHAT ARE THE MENSHEVIKS LEADERS PREPARED FOR?

THE LEADERS IN EXILE DEFINE THEIR POSITION AT A GENEVA PARTY CONFERENCE, APRIL 1905.

THE WORKERS ARE SPLIT AND **CAN DO NOTHING**... ONLY THE ORGANIZED LIBERAL BOURGEOISIE CAN CONFRONT TSARISM...

OUR TASK IS TO GIVE THE LIBERALS **COURAGE** ... BUT ON NO ACCOUNT MUST WE **FRIGHTEN** THEM BY MAKING **PROLETARIAN DEMANDS**...

SHOULD THE **BOURGEOIS REVOLUTION** SUCCEED IN SETTING UP A PARLIAMENT, WE SHOULD **NOT** SHARE POWER BUT REMAIN A **PARTY OF OPPOSITION**...

AXELROD

PLEKHANOV

MARTYNOV

HOW CAN YOU WIN - IF YOU'RE AIMING <u>NOT</u> TO ?

"How can you count on the liberal bourgeoisie? Their struggle for liberty will be half-hearted. Their **property, status** and **class interests** are tied up with the existing social order. Therefore, they will seek a **constitutional compromise** which will not overthrow Tsarism or prevent it from crushing the **peasant-proletarian movement!**"

The Bolshevik 3rd Congress of the RSDLP...

Reports are heard on the size and kind of Bolshevik membership (12 thousand, 60% proletarian, 17 Party cells in the Petersburg factories, etc.)

The trouble starts when Lenin and Bogdanov propose a resolution to admit a **majority of workers** on each local committee . . .

Lenin is booed, attacked, and **What Is To Be Done?** is quoted against him.

Lenin is outvoted! Why? Because the local committee-men (komitetchiki) are loyal to the concept of an **illegal underground** Party. But Lenin foresees that the **partial** success of the revolution may result in a need to work **legally,** above ground.

Frightened by the strikes, mutinies and uprisings, the Tsar offers the bourgeoisie an **Imperial Duma** (parliament). But it's only for the **rich** voting for the rich – and it fools no one!

Then in October the Bolshevik printers in Moscow go on strike (demanding the same pay for punctuation marks as for letters!) The strike spreads into ...

The biggest General Strike in labour history!

HOWEVER ... the **bourgeois nature** of the revolution is clear: The liberal Kadet party, professionals and industrialists **support** the strike. Employers give their strikers **half** or **full pay** ...

... the revolution is **limited** to the collision between the capitalist forces of production and an outmoded Tsarist administration ... and limited to a **minimum programme** of democratic goals (a republic, economic reforms, separation of church and state, land reforms, etc.)

"The degree of Russia's economic development (an objective condition), and the degree of class-consciousness and organization of the broad masses of the proletariat (a subjective condition inseparably bound up with the objective condition) make the immediate and complete emancipation of the working class impossible."　**Lenin**

...Proletarian Democracy: ⋙→

On Oct. 13th the **Soviet** (it means 'Council') of Workers' Representatives of St. Petersburg is founded. By **whom?** By worker-delegates elected on the basis of one for every 500 workers. The Soviet is genuinely **proletarian**: its Menshevik affiliation is strong. But neither Mensheviks, SRs nor Bolsheviks control it.

THE SOVIET...

The Soviet lasts only 50 days. But it advances the example of workers' democracy far beyond the Paris Commune of 1871.

Strikes are always important because by their **withdrawal** of labour the workers **recognize** their power. But a general strike means **total withdrawal**, which makes it necessary for workers themselves to organize the continuity of society, and this experience provides a first real recognition of **workers' self-government**.

THE EXILES RETURN AND PREPARE FOR COMBAT UNITY...

Trotsky arrives in Russia disguised as an eye patient and is helped by **Krassin**.

Krasin and **Bogdanov** want to negotiate Party unity with the Mensheviks. **Lenin** agrees to a joint unifying 4th Congress.

Parvus, with Trotsky, runs the Menshevik paper **Nachalo**. Parvus (A.L.Helfand 1869-1924) a Russian exile active on the German SDP left. He ends up a right-wing supporter of Germany during the First World War.

Trotsky (alias 'Yanovsky') leads the Mensheviks and is appointed Chairman of the Soviet Executive Committee. **Martov** is the only other Menshevik leader in Russia in 1905.

HMMM, THAT TROTSKY — HE'S MORE OF A BOLSHEVIK THAN HE REALIZES!

Lenin is delayed in Stockholm and arrives (disguised as 'Karpov') after the Soviet is set up. With **Maxim Gorky** and **Litvinov**, he edits the Bolshevik paper **Novaya Zhizn** (New Life).

Lenin is unhappy about the progress of the Combat Committee which he now heads: "There's been **talk** about bombs for over 6 months — yet not one has been made!"

"Go to the youth, gentlemen! That is the only remedy! Otherwise – I give you my word for it – you will be left with 'learned' memoranda, plans, charts, schemes, and magnificent recipes, but without an organization, without a living cause . . ."

LENIN VERSUS TROSTKY ... OPPOSING ⟫⟶

Lenin's concept of bourgeois revolution:

. . . the **people** (proletariat and peasants) are the decisive force which will topple Tsarism.

Trotsky's concept of permanent revolution:

. . . if the revolution depends on the proletariat, why shouldn't it **keep on going** straight into socialism without imposing a bourgeois-democratic limit on itself?

If this democratic revolution **succeeds**, we can begin to pass to the socialist revolution. We stand for **uninterrupted revolution.**

But only the proletariat **in power,** as the **leading class,** can finally emancipate the peasants through socialism.

VIEWS ON 'BOURGEOIS' REVOLUTION

FINALLY, YES ...BUT IN IN THE **MEANTIME**...

.. a bourgeois revolution, backed by a **resolute** proletariat/peasant alliance, might introduce **nationalization of the land** as a basis for industrial progress. But nationalization doesn't mean **socialism** or even equal land tenure.

Proletarian revolution in a backward country like Russia cannot succeed **on its own** without the support of **international** revolutions in more advanced countries.

THAT'S TRUE, **BUT...**

The development of capitalism proceeds extremely **unevenly** in different countries. From this it follows irrefutably that socialism cannot achieve victory simultaneously **in all** countries. It will achieve victory first in one or several countries, while the others will for some time remain bourgeois or pre-bourgeois.

Trotsky's idea of **permanent revolution** and Lenin's **uninterrupted revolution** are based on Marx ...

While the democratic petty bourgeois wish to bring the revolution to a conclusion as quickly as possible ... it is our task to make the revolution **permanent**, until all more or less possessing classes have been displaced from domination, until the proletariat has conquered state power, and the association of the proletarians, not only in one country but in all the dominant countries of the world, has advanced so far that competition among the proletarians of these countries has ceased and that at least the decisive productive forces are concentrated in the hands of the proletarians.
Marx, **Address to the Communist League,** 1850.

LENIN'S VISION OF WORKERS' POWER...

IN STOCKHOLM, BEFORE ARRIVING BACK IN **RUSSIA**, LENIN WROTE AN OPEN LETTER* TO **NOVAYA ZHIZN**:

LENIN'S IMPORTANT LETTER WAS **NOT PRINTED** BY THE PAPER!

OUR PETERSBURG BOLSHEVIKS ARE WRONG IF THEY TRY TO FORCE THE SOVIETS TO ACCEPT **OUR** PARTY PROGRAMME AND **OUR** LEADERSHIP.

...DO NOT ATTEMPT TO **LIMIT** THE SOVIET TO OUR PARTY MEMBERS ...THE SOVIETS MUS RECRUIT NON-PARTY WORKER SAILORS, SOLDIERS, PEASANTS, AND BOURGEOIS INTELLECTUALS

...LET THE SOVIET UNITE THESE **MIXED DEMOCRATIC** ELEMENTS... OTHERWISE THE REVOLUTION WILL **FAIL!**

...THE SOVIET ISN'T JUST A 'STRIKE COMMITTEE' IT IS A **PROVISIONAL REVOLUTIONAR** GOVERNMENT!

IT IS THE FUTURE FORM OF WORKERS' DEMOCRACY!

LENIN WAS **ALONE** IN **SEEING** THE HISTORICAL ROLE OF THE SOVIETS.

Why did the 1905 revolution fail?

When the workers in Moscow and Petersburg continued to strike in November for an 8-hour day, the big employers **withdrew their support** — and so did liberals, like **Milyukov** and **Struve**.

In fact, withdrawal of democratic bourgeois support began on Oct. 30th when the clever **Count Witte** convinced the Tsar to declare **amnesty**, a **constitution** and a **Duma** (parliament) . . .

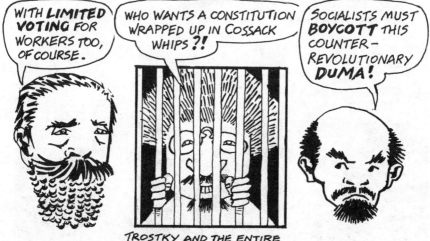

TROSTKY AND THE ENTIRE PETERSBURG SOVIET EXECUTIVE ARE ARRESTED DEC. 16.

...THE ARMY STILL

...THE WORKERS OF THE KRASNAYA PRESNYA DISTRICT RESIST BRAVELY...

BARRICADES ARE NO MATCH FOR LONG-RANGE ARTILLERY!

THE BOLSHEVIK-LED UPRISING, MOSCOW DEC. 9~31...

THE STRIKE WAS **UNTIMELY.** THE WORKERS SHOULD NOT HAVE TAKEN TO ARMS

WE SHOULD HAVE EXPLAINED TO THE MASSES THAT IT WAS IMPOSSIBLE TO CONFINE THINGS TO A PEACEFUL STRIKE AND THAT A FEARLESS AND RELENTLESS **ARMED FIGHT** WAS NECESSARY

Plekhanov was not in Russia in 1905.

OBEYS THE TSAR...

...ACROSS RUSSIA, FIRING SQUADS, COURT MARTIALS, MASS FLOGGINGS AND ARRESTS FINISH THE REVOLUTION, JANUARY 1906.
TROSTKY and PARVUS GET LIFE SENTENCES IN SIBERIA (BUT SOON ESCAPE).

TROTSKY IN PRISON

1905 has proven 3 things

1

a transfer of **state power** to the bourgeoisie cannot happen peacefully, as the Menshevik leaders hoped.

2

the Menshevik **leaders** have proven themselves anti-revolutionary . . . but the rank-and-file Menshevik **workers** and Bolsheviks in the Soviet were united by the armed uprising.

3

the experience of 1905 proves that the Soviets of Workers' Deputies are **organs of direct mass struggle**. It was not some theory, not appeals on the part of someone, tactics invented by someone, not party doctrine, but the force of circumstances that led these non-party mass organs to realize the need for an uprising . . .
However . . . it is also true that Soviets are not sufficient for organizing the **immediate fighting force**, for **organizing an uprising** in the narrowest sense of the word.

Lenin attended the 4th and 5th Unity Congresses, only leaving Russia finally in 1907. One moonlit December night, Lenin set off across the frozen Finnish channel 2 miles to a ship headed for Stockholm . . . **the ice began cracking** — like the RSDLP Party itself!

WHAT A STUPID WAY TO DIE!...

4th ALL-PARTY CONGRESS IN STOCKHOLM, April 4–25, 1906

...ATTENDED BY BUNDISTS - BOLSHEVIKS - MENSHEVIKS - LATVIAN POLISH AND UKRAINIAN SOCIAL-DEMOCRATS

IN THE MARCH 1906 ELECTIONS TO THE DUMA, THE KADETS GAIN 153 SEATS, AND THE TRUDOVIKS (A NEW PEASANT LABOUR PARTY) GAIN 94.

THE MENSHEVIKS WHO HAVE 19 SEATS PROPOSE AN ALLIANCE WITH THE KADETS

LENIN ARGUES FOR A 'LEFT-BLOC' WITH SRS AND TRUDOVIKS

OTHER BOLSHEVIKS DEMAND A BOYCOTT OF THE DUMA...

... BUT LENIN SURPRISES THEM BY VOTING FOR PARTICIPATION

5th CONGRESS IN LONDON,
April 30 – May 19, 1907

AT THIS LAST BIG 'UNITY' CONGRESS LENIN REGAINS
A MAJORITY ON THE **RSDLP** CENTRAL COMMITTEE

IN THE 1907 2nd **DUMA** THE **RSDLP** HAS
65 SEATS INCLUDING 18 BOLSHEVIKS
BUT THE BOLSHEVIKS FACTION OF
'**BOYCOTTISTS**' CONTINUE TO ATTACK LENIN

THE 'DUMA QUESTION' SPLITS UP THE RSDLP...
THE DARK, BITTER YEARS 1906-11 NEARLY DESTROY THE PARTY...

THE STOLYPIN REGIME 1906-1911

3 JUNE 1907
STOLYPIN DISSOLVES BOTH THE 1ST AND 2ND DUMAS DECREES **NEW ELECTION LAWS.** THIS MEANS THE PEASANTS' VOTE IS CUT BY HALF, WORKERS' BY ONE-THIRD. SO THE 3RD DUMA IS PACKED WITH CONSERVATIVE BOURGEOIS AND LANDOWNERS...

P.A. STOLYPIN (1862-1911) NEW MINISTER OF THE INTERIOR AFTER WITTE (AND LIKE PLEHVE, ASSASSINATED IN A 'DOUBLE AGENT' PLOT)...

RECALLISTS OR OTZOVISTS
1908: the Boycottist leader, Bogdanov, and others demand that Bolshevik Duma deputies be **recalled** for not carrying out party directives.

BOYCOTTISTS
1907: the majority of Bolshevik leaders favour a **boycott** of the 3rd Duma.

ULTIMATISTS
these Bolsheviks demand that the deputies either carry out party directives or resign from the Duma

TO HELL WITH THIS COMIC-OPERA DUMA!

CALL 'EM BACK!

EITHER—OR ELSE!

KAMENEV

BOGDANOV

ALEXINSKY

STOLYPIN'S MASTERPIECE: AGRARIAN REFORMS WHICH OUTLIVE HIM

...THE VILLAGE COMMUNE (OBSHCHINA) IS ABOLISHED. BETWEEN 1907-16 OVER 6 MILLION PEASANT FAMILIES BECOME **INDIVIDUAL LANDOWNERS.** STOLYPIN'S REFORMS ARE DESIGNED TO CREATE A CONSERVATIVE, PROPERTY-MINDED CLASS OF **KULAKS** WHO WILL SUPPORT THE STATE...

WE HAVE NO CHOICE BUT TO WORK **INSIDE** THIS DUMA PIGSTY!

LIQUIDATORS

1908-1912: Mensheviks and right-ing SRs call for an end to all legal underground action in favour legal work in trade unions and operatives.

PARTYITES

1909: splinter faction of the Mensheviks led by Plekhanov which cooperates briefly with Lenin against the Liquidators.

LET'S GO STRAIGHT!

VPERYODISTS

1909: coalition of Recallists and Ultimatists grouped round the publication of **Vperyod** against Lenin's new underground paper **Proletarii** (1906)

CONCILIATORS

from 1904 on: a 'non-factional' attempt, led by Trotsky, to reconcile the warring wings of Russian Social-Democracy.

MARTOV

GORKY

PLEKHANOV

TROTSKY

99

A QUESTION OF ILLEGAL FINANCES

Full-time Party members got an average worker's wage (30 rubles a month or less). Where did the Party finances come from? From 'angels' – rich sympathizers like 'Auntie' Kalmykova who financed **Iskra** or the textile tycoon S. T. Morozov, a pro-Bolshevik said to have committed suicide after 1905. Morozov's nephew, N. P. Schmidt (financed **Novaya Zhizn**) was tortured and murdered by the police, but he left his estate to the Bolsheviks.

Still **more** finances were urgently needed. So Lenin goes ahead with **expropriations**, or 'exes', armed robberies of banks.

25 June 1907, Bolshevik agents led by **Kamo** (S.A. Ter-Petrossian, 1882-1922) raid the Tiflis Treasury and get away with 341,000 rubles.

THE 'EXPROPRIATIONS' SCANDAL...

Both Mensheviks and Bolsheviks criticize Lenin at the Stockholm and London Congresses.

One of the chief organizers of the 'exes' at the 1907 London Congress . . .

STALIN

Born Joseph Djugashvili (1879-1953) the son of a poor Georgian shoemaker, ex-seminary student, a Bolshevik since 1904, arrested and exiled to Siberia six times, rises to the Bolshevik Central Committee 1912.

The Intra-Party Struggle

Bogdanov's claim as ideological defender of 'pure' Bolshevism is backed by his new philosophy, **Empiriomonism**, based on **Mach** and **neo-Kantianism**, already adopted by the **revisionist** Marxists in Germany and Austria. **Fideism** attracts Gorky and Lunacharsky.

In 1909, Bogdanov, Lunacharsky and other ultra-leftists organize an Otzovisty (Recallist) school at Gorky's villa on Capri.

THE CAPRI SCHOOL ARE FISHING IN POLLUTED WATERS... RELIGION, METAPHYSICS, REVISIONISM... DRAGGING EVERY KIND OF FAD AND FASHION INTO MARXISM...

MACH

FIDEISM: ATTEMPT TO RESCUE RELIGION AND MYSTICISM FOR THE 'BENEFIT' OF SOCIALISM

EMPIRIO-CRITICISM: POSITIVIST PHILOSOPHY FOUNDED BY ERNST MACH (1838-1916) - RICHARD AVENARIUS (1843-1896) ATTEMPTS TO COMBINE PHYSICS WITH PSYCHOLOGY AND RESTRICT SCIENTIFIC THEORY TO DESCRIPTIONS OF SENSE-DATA

extends to philosophy...

Lenin launches his counter-attack, Materialism and Empirio-Criticism in 1908.

And at an editorial conference of the Bolshevik paper **Proletarii**, in Paris, 1909, Lenin expels Bogdanov from the Party.

Bogdanov was not active in the 1917 Revolution: but he founded the **Proletcult** movement. His experiments in **blood-transfusion** led to his death.

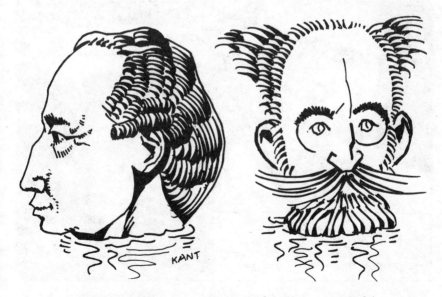

KANT

NEO-KANTIANISM: KNOWLEDGE OF REALITY IS **RELATIVE**, LIMITED AND CONDITIONED BY THE MIND

REVISIONISM: IS NEO-KANTIANISM APPLIED TO SOCIALISM. BERNSTEIN: "THE MOVEMENT IS EVERYTHING, THE ULTIMATE AIM IS NOTHING"

The dark night of exile life...

After the failure of 1905, despair, apathy, illness, poverty, suicide, madness and police spies haunt the exiles. The terrible darkness is summed up by the **Lafargues'** double suicide (Marx's daughter and son-in-law) in 1911. Lenin attends their funeral in Paris.

I MAY NOT LIVE TO SEE THE REVOLUTION...

G. Y. ZINOVIEV
(1883-1936) THEORETICIAN AND BOLSHEVIK LOYAL TO LENIN, ELECTED TO CENTRAL COMMITTEE IN 1907.

IN 1911, WITH ZINOVIEV AND KAMENEV, LENIN ESTABLISHES A SCHOOL FOR UNDERGROUND PARTY WORKERS AT LONGJUMEAU OUTSIDE PARIS...

Inessa Armand, born Elizabeth De Herbenville, 1875, of French theatre folk settled in Russia. She married a textile manufacturer and had 5 children. Became a radical feminist and Bolshevik organizer, twice arrested in 1905 and 1907, and escaped from Siberia. Member of the Soviet Executive Committee, 1917. She died in 1920 of typhus in the North Caucasus.

SIGH!

Inessa's death was a deep personal tragedy for Lenin.

KRUPSKAYA WAS WELL AWARE OF LENIN'S PASSION...

ALEXANDRA KOLLONTAI (1872-1952) DAUGHTER OF A TSARIST GENERAL, ACTIVIST, FEMINIST, COMMISSAR FOR PUBLIC WELFARE IN 1917.

1912... the Bolsheviks revive

AT A CONFERENCE HELD IN PRAGUE, JANUARY 19-30, 1912, THE BOLSHEVIK 'HARDS' RALLY ROUND LENIN...

Y.M. SVERDLOV

(1885-1919) from a poor Nizhni-Novgorod artisan family, pharmacist, militant organizer working illegally since 1903, arrested 5 times, future first President of the Soviet Republic.

N.I. BUKHARIN

(1888-1938) parents are Moscow school-teachers, chief Bolshevik theorist, student organizer. Future Politburo member, head of the Comintern, and for 3 years co-leader with Stalin of the Communist Party.

STALIN

S.G. SHAUMYAN

(1878-1918) Bolshevik since 1903, Party organizer in Georgia. One of the 26 People's Commissars of Baku. Executed by the British Expeditionary Forces in 1918.

OUR TOUGHEST UNDERGROUND ORGANIZERS ARE ALL YOUNG MEN...

THE BOLSHEVIKS ORGANIZE A 'LEGAL' DAILY **PRAVDA** (TRUTH) IN
ST. PETERSBURG • **PRAVDA** HAS TO CHANGE ITS NAME 8 TIMES...

V.M. MOLOTOV ⟫⟫→

(Born 1890) son of a Kirov village shop-
clerk, Bolshevik since 1906, secretary of
Pravda editorial board. Future USSR
Minister for Foreign Affairs.

July 1912, Lenin moves party headquarters
to Cracow, Poland, to direct **Pravda** and the
4th Duma elections . . .
. . . only 6 Bolsheviks re-enter the Duma
(Nov.28). But, because of Stolypin's
undemocratic reforms, this represents 88% of
the workers' electors, while the 7 Mensheviks
represent only 11%.

 ⟫⟫→

6000 miners in the Lena goldfields (Siberia)
strike . . .
4 April 1912, the police massacre 500 strikers
which sparks off protest strikes across
Russia . . .

August 1st 1914...

...ON JUNE 28, 1914, SERBIAN NATIONALISTS ASSASSINATE THE AUSTRIAN ARCHDUKE FRANZ FERDINAND AND HIS WIFE AT SARAVEJO...

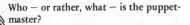

Who — or rather, what — is the puppet-master?

The first 14-odd years of the 20th century were marked by **imperialist, colony-grabbing wars**: the Spanish-American War 1898, the Boer War 1899-1902, the Russo-Japanese War 1905, the Italo-Turkish War 1911-12, the Balkan Wars 1912-13, etc.

This un-declared 'cold war' between rival imperialist nations finally becomes **red hot** in 1914!

108

he First War World begins

LENIN IS ARRESTED AS AN ENEMY ALIEN IN POLISH AUSTRIA, AUGUST 7th

Victor Adler, leading Austrian Social-Democrat, secures his release from prison, and Lenin takes refuge in neutral Switzerland on the 23rd August.

THE OUTBREAK OF WAR IS NO SURPRISE...

BOOM!

BOOM!

...BUT SOMETHING ELSE IS...

The collapse of the

Voting for the budget means voting for the war!

Like **Plekhanov**, socialist leaders in Germany, France, Belgium etc., became 'defensists' and supporters of 'patriotic war'. Others, like **Trotsky, Martov, Axelrod**, remained faithful to the struggle for international peace.

Gustav Noske (1868-1946) a right-wing German Social-Democrat, later organized the suppression of the German workers' revolution in 1918-21 and his officers murdered the founders of the German Communist Party, Luxemburg and Liebknecht.

Benito Mussolini (1883-1945) was expelled from the Italian Socialist Party for his pro-war views. In 1919 he organized Fascism.

Rosa Luxemburg (1871-1919) and **Karl Liebknecht** (1871-1919) were left-wing German Social-Democrats.

Delegates from 25 nations, at the 1907 Stuttgart International Congress and again at the 1912 Basle Congress, had accepted 'Red Rosa's resolution:
1)   to **prevent war** by any means
2)   or if they could not prevent it, to turn the crisis caused by war into a **revolution**

Only one leader in the 2nd International lived up to the second pledge — **Lenin!**

111

PEACEFUL SOCIALISM?

'PHILOSOPHERS HAVE ONLY INTERPRETED THE WORLD IN VARIOUS WAYS: THE POINT IS TO CHANGE IT.'

XI th THESIS ON FEUERBACH KARL MARX 1844

MARX 'PEACEFULLY' AT WORK IN THE BRITISH MUSEUM LIBRARY

MARX'S FAMOUS **XI th THESIS** IS THE ESSENCE OF **PROLETARIAN** PHILOSOPHY...

ENGELS

...IT CALLS FOR **ACTION** NOT CONTEMPLATION!

ROSA

But the 2nd International operated in a **peaceful** period of European history (1889-1914). Many socialists began thinking that 'revolution' was no longer their **immediate** business . . . and they began to interpret Marx "in various ways" (economism, reformism, revisionism etc.) . . .

...FORGETTING THAT IT'S THE **WORLD** THEY MUST CHANGE – NOT MARX!

On the consequences of peaceful socialism

The West entered a phase of 'peaceful'
preparations for the changes to come.
Socialist parties, basically proletarian, were
formed everywhere, and learned to use
bourgeois parliamentarism and to found their
own daily press, their educational institutions,
their trade unions and their cooperative
societies . . .
The dialectics of history were such that the
theoretical victory of Marxism compelled its
enemies to **disguise themselves** as Marxists.
Liberalism, rotten within, tried to revive itself
in the form of socialist **opportunism** . . . They
cravenly preached 'social peace' (i.e., peace
with the slave-owners), renunciation of the
class struggle, etc. They had very many
adherents among socialist members of
parliament, various officials of the working-
class movement, and the 'sympathising'
intelligentsia.

    Lenin, **Pravda** No.50, 1913.
    On the 30th anniversary of Marx's death

LENIN 'PEACEFULLY' AT WORK IN
THE BERNE LIBRARY, SWITZERLAND

...WRITES *IMPERIALISM, THE*
HIGHEST STAGE OF
CAPITALISM, 1915-16

...THE 'PEACEFUL'
PHASE IS OVER!

WHY IS IMPERIALISM THE 'HIGHEST STAGE' OF CAPITALISM?

Marx studied capitalism in its early stage of **free competition** and **world-market expansion**. But, around 1900, the struggle to dominate the world-market increases . . . and 'free enterpri capitalism.turns into **monopoly** capitalism.

WHAT IS MONOPOLY CAPITALISM?

Essentially, it is a link-up between high finance, big industry and the national government.

More and more, the national economy is **directed** by the monopoly system which controls large holdings of shares.

Stocks, shares and state loans increase the amount and power of **surplus-capital**.

This surplus-capital is **exported** beyond the national borders as investments and loans to 'backward' countries.

A struggle develops between the **supra-** or **multi**-national monopolies to control the world-market.

But since the world has already been divided up by the imperial Great Powers, the rival monopolists struggle to **re-partition** the wor — to 'muscle in'.

Therefore . . .

The **economic disparity** between rival monopolists — and the **uneven development** of rival capitalist nations — make imperialist wars inevitable . . .

"The European and world war has the clearly defined character of a **bourgeois, imperialist** ar **dynastic** war. A struggle for markets and for freedom to look foreign countries, a striving to suppress the revolutionary movement of the proletariat and democracy in the individual countries, a desire to deceive, disunite, and slaughter the proletarians of all countries by setti the wage slaves of one nation against those of another so as to benefit the bourgeoisie — thes are the only real content and significance of the war."

HOW'S THE WAR 'DOING'?

WAR IS THE ULTIMATE, AND DEADLIEST CONTEST BETWEEN COMPETITIVE 'BRAND NAMES'...

IS THIS A WAR... OR AN **ADVERTISING CAMPAIGN** BETWEEN RIVAL ARMS MANUFACTURERS?!?

THE WAR HAS ARMED WORKERS **EITHER** TO KILL EACH OTHER IN THE INTERESTS OF THE BOURGEOISIE - **OR** TO SMASH THE STATE!

TURN THE WAR INTO CIVIL WAR!... AND THE

THERE IS NO QUESTION OF
WORKERS 'WINNING' THIS WAR...

...THE TWO SIDES ARE 'BOTH WORSE'
...SOCIALISTS MUST WORK FOR THE
DEFEAT OF **ALL** THEIR OWN
COUNTRIES!

FIRST STEP IS REVOLUTIONARY DEFEATISM... 117

WHAT IS 'REVOLUTIONARY DEFEATISM'?

War identifies the State with Society ~ Revolution identifies the class war within society...

In time of war, everyone has to **identify** with the State . . . everyone, no matter from what **class**, has to defend the State, the 'Fatherland'.

To go against your government is 'defeatism' — it is **treason** against the State!

But is your country in danger? or the ruling class? The ruling class alone controls the State and identifies **all of society** with its **own** class interests.

Are the workers defending their **own** interests, their **own** state, their **own** class in the front-line trenches?

Workers of **all** countries can only gain from the defeat of all their 'own' countries.

Defeat makes it easier to turn the world war into **civil war** between hostile classes — and into a world-wide revolution!

LENIN'S UPHILL STRUGGLE 1915·1917

On Sept. 5th, 1915, a conference of 38 anti-war socialists meets at Zimmerwald, a Swiss village.
Lenin's theses on **revolutionary defeatism** and **civil war** gain only left-wing minority support.
But the Conference majority doesn't want to break with the International. Trotsky's proposal, "peace without victors or vanquished", is adopted as the **Zimmerwald Manifesto** by the French, German, Italian and Menshevik majority, May 1915.
For Lenin, **pacifism** and **defence of the Fatherland** are equally betrayals of the class struggle.

At the next anti-war conference at Kienthal, April 1916, support for Lenin increases. By 1917 Lenin has attracted a growing number of non-Russian followers who will act as members of the **3rd Communist International!**

AND THE BOLSHEVIKS ?

On August 8th, 1914, both Menshevik and Bolshevik RSDLP deputies in the Duma **abstained** from voting for the **war budget** (which is passed anyway by the rest of the Duma).

But Lenin's **defeatism** policy seems "hard to swallow" and was not accepted by the Bolshevik Central Committee — including even the loyal Kamenev.

The arrest and Siberian exile of 5 Bolshevik deputies and other leaders disrupts the Party organization. But **rank-and-file** Bolshevik **workers** organize an increasing number of anti-war strikes between 1915-17.

In 1915 the first mass 'defeatist' surrenders occur at the front. The sailors of the Baltic fleet mutiny. By 1917 some 15 million workers and peasants are in uniform . . . a **revolutionary tidal wave!**

THE TSAR'S 'WEDDING~CAKE' FALLS TO BITS...

NICKIE DEAR, DO AS 'OUR FRIEND' SAYS...

The Tsar and Tsarina's 'friend' is **Grigori Rasputin** (1871-1916) Siberian peasant monk, horse-thief and charlatan. He uses hypnotism to control the Tsarevich's haemophiliac attacks of bleeding.

The Tsarina's blind faith in the shrewd miracle-man gives him great power to interfere at the Imperial Court.

SUPERSTITION

DECADENCE

CORRUPTION

INCOMPETENCE

CONSPIRACY

Generals, nobles and politicians talk openly now of a coup d'etat as approved by French and British diplomats.

FEBRUARY 1917... IN THE STREETS, ⋙

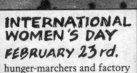

INTERNATIONAL WOMEN'S DAY FEBRUARY 23rd.
hunger-marchers and factory workers clash with the police

FEBRUARY 24th.
200,000 workers on strike in Petrograd

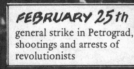

FEBRUARY 25th
general strike in Petrograd, shootings and arrests of revolutionists

FEBRUARY 26th.
Duma dissolved by the Tsar: but the deputies decide to meet 'unofficially'

FEBRUARY 27th
mutiny of the guard regiments and formation of the Soviet of Workers' Deputies. The Duma forms a 'provisional committee'

FEBRUARY 28th
the Tsar's Ministers arrested and the Schlusselberg Prison captured by workers and soldiers. First issue of **Izvestiia**

17

18-го Апрѣля 1917

THE PEOPLE OVERTHROW TSARISM...

Да здравствуетъ соціализмъ

РАБ.ОБ.МАСТ... ...НСТИТ.

MARCH 1st

Formation of the soldiers'
section of the Soviet and first
session of the Moscow
Soviet . . .

къ 1-го Мая
етроградѣ.

Дворцовая площадь

BUT WHO HAS THE POWER?

THE PEOPLE MAY GO TOO FAR!

V.M. Chernov, a leader of the SR Party and Soviet delegate accepts a cabinet post in the Provisional Government, May 4th.

A.F. Kerensky, lawyer, SR leader and Trudovik deputy in the 1912 4th Duma, elected vice-chairman of the Soviet. March 3rd he becomes Minister of Justice in the Provisional Government, later War Minister, and finally head of government, May 17th.

EVERYONE'S BUSY ABDICATING... INCLUDING THE SOCIALIST LEADERS OF THE SOVIET!

THE FEBRUARY REVOLUTION CONTAINS THE SEEDS OF A BOURGEOIS COUNTER-REVOLUTION!

The bourgeoisie who hate the revolution have been dragged into it by the hair! But the 'moderate' socialists cling to the dogmatic belief that the revolution must be bourgeois. However, the Soviet leaders cannot support a bourgeois government without going against the will of a revolutionary majority, against the fact that a workers' republic already exists!

125

HOW DID 'DUAL POWER' ARISE?

SOLDIERS' DELEGATES IN THE DUMA (TAURIDE PALACE) WHERE THE PROVISIONAL GOVERNMENT AND THE SOVIET **BOTH** MEET.

AFTER ALL, SOLDIERS ARE **PEASANTS IN UNIFORM!**

YES... BUT WHO **REPRESENTS** YOU IN THE SOVIET?

Mainly the petty-bourgeois socialist SR party — the largest in the Soviet — which has attracted masses of peasants, shopkeepers, professionals, landowners, officers . . . and even some generals!

'An attitude of unreasoning trust in the capitalists . . . characterizes the politics of the **popular masses** in Russia at the present moment; this is the fruit that has grown with revolutionary rapidity on the social and economic soil of the most petty-bourgeois of all European countries. This is the **class** basis for the 'agreement' between the provisional government and the Soviet . . .'

TO MAKE THINGS WORSE, THE BOLSHEVIK LEADERSHIP IS
DISUNIFIED AND CONFUSED...

MARCH 12th KAMENEV, MURANOV (FORMER DUMA DEPUTY)
AND STALIN, BACK FROM SIBERIA, RESUME THE
EDITORSHIP OF **PRAVDA**.

Lenin in Zurich...

During the war Zurich was a refuge for pacificists, spies, deserters, black-market racketeers . . . and a new, bizarre art-form named DADA . . .

GADJI BERI BIMBA

TRISTAN TZARA
RUMANIAN 'DADA'
IMPRESARIO

HUGO BALL
GERMAN 'DADA' POET

ONE SHOULD ALWAYS TRY TO BE AS **RADICAL** AS REALITY ITSELF...

7-26 MARCH, LENIN WRITES **5 LETTERS FROM AFAR** . . .

The proletariat . . . if it wants to uphold the gains of the present revolution and proceed further, to win peace, bread and freedom, must 'smash', to use Marx's expression, the bourgeois 'ready-made' state machine and substitute a new one for it by **merging** the police force, the army and the bureaucracy with the **entire armed people** . . .

from the 3rd **Letter** (but only the 1st was published by **Pravda**!)

128

Martov's plan is to gain permits to cross Germany in a 'sealed train' in exchange for German and Austrian prisoners of war in Russia.

[Parus contacts the German Generals . . .]

March 27th: Lenin and 32 Bolsheviks cross Germany in a **sealed train** . . . Martov and many other exiles followed in the next few months.

THE FINLAND STATION...APRIL 3rd 1917

Lenin arrives at the 'Tsar's station' in the Vyborg district and is met by the Petrograd Soviet leaders and thousands of Bolshevik workers and soldiers . . .

nd that same evening
n's "thunder-like speech"
ks SRs, Mensheviks and
loyal Bolsheviks . . .

On April 4th Lenin presents his ideas to the Party Conference. This is one of the most important documents of the revolution:

THE APRIL THESES

1

... the new government of Milyukov and Co. pursues an imperialist war owing to its capitalist nature. On our part, not the slightest concession to 'revolutionary defensism' is permissible...

2

... the country is **passing** from the first stage of the revolution — which owing to the insufficient class-consciousness and organization of the proletariat, placed power in the hands of the bourgeoisie — to its **second** stage, which must place power in the hands of the proletariat and poorest sections of the peasants ...

3

No support for the provisional government ... an end to the impermissible, illusion-breeding 'demand' that **this** government, a government of capitalists, should cease to be an imperialist government ...

4

The masses must be made to see that the Soviets of Worker's Deputies are the **only possible** form of revulutionary government ... our task is (so long as we are in the minority) to present a patient, systematic, and persistent explanation adapted to the practical needs of the masses ...

5

. . . to return to a parliamentary republic from the Soviets of Workers' Deputies would be a retrograde step . . .

Abolition of the police, the army and the bureaucracy. The Salaries of all officials . . . not to exceed the average wage of a competent worker.

6

Confiscation of all landed estates.
Nationalization of **all** lands in the country . . . The organization of separate Soviets of Deputies of Poor Peasants. The setting up of a model farm on each of the large estates . . .

7

The immediate amalgamation of all banks in the country into a single national bank, and the institution of control over it by the Soviet . . .

8

It is not our **immediate** task to 'introduce' socialism, but only to bring social production and the distribution of products at once under the **control** of the Soviets . . .

ON APRIL 8th THE PETERSBURG BOLSHEVIK COMMITTEE REJECTS LENIN'S **APRIL THESES** BY 13 VOTES TO 2. (AND THE SOVIET AND DUMA LEADERS ARE **DELIGHTED!**)

LENIN HAD **NO** SUPPORT FROM THE BOLSHEVIK LEADERSHIP...

LENIN'S ALL WASHED UP!

HE WILL BE - IF HE DOESN'T **CALM DOWN**

KOLLONTAI (UNTIL THEN A MENSHEVIK)

CHERNOV SR

MILIUKOV KADET

133

LENIN STRUGGLES TO CONVINCE THE 'OLD BOLSHEVIKS'...

LENIN'S SUDDEN **COMPLETE BREAK** WITH THE ACCEPTED DOCTRINE OF BOURGEOIS REVOLUTION CONFUSED THE 'OLD GUARD'...

LENIN'S **THESES** ARE ... PERPLEXING!

HOW CAN HE SAY THE BOURGEOIS REVOLUTION IS **COMPLETED**?!

IT HASN'T EVEN STARTED ON THE **MINIMUM PROGRAMME** ...

WHERE ARE LENIN'S **FACTS**?

ZINOVIEV

KAMENEV

RYKOV

STALIN

Lenin patiently explains...

1. The passing of state power from one **class** to another is the first, the principal, the basic sign of a **revolution**, both in the strictly scientific and in the practical political meaning of that term.

2. The revolutionary-democratic dictatorship of the proletariat and peasants has **already** become a reality in the Russian revolution ... it is a power directly based on revolutionary seizure, on the direct initiative of the people from below, and **not on a law** enacted by a centralized state power.

DO YOU REALLY BELIEVE THAT THIS **POWER FROM THE PEOPLE** SHOULD BE HANDED OVER TO THE BOURGEOISIE?

134

AND PATIENTLY EXPLAIN...

In the next few months, Lenin regained total party support, while Bolshevik militants went on "patiently explaining" his ideas to the workers . . .

PARTY MEMBERSHIP WENT UP FROM 24,000 IN FEBRUARY TO 240,000 BY JULY!

LENIN - AND **ONLY** LENIN - COULD **RE-ARM** THE PARTY **IDEOLOGICALLY!**

SVERDLOV
Head of the Party Centre Secretariat which has to cope with the huge increase.

Trotsky arrives May 17th, joins Lenin, and is elected to the Bolshevik Central Committee in August.

135

'REVOLUTIONARY DEFENSISM'

THE SLOGAN OF PETTY BOURGEOIS SOCIALISM!

The provisional government is under pressure from the Allies to **continue** the war. With the support of 'defensist' SR and Menshevik leaders in the Soviet, Kerensky orders a Russian offensive in Galicia, June 16th.

By 1917 the army is disintegrating (with nearly 8 million dead or wounded) and between June-October, 2 million soldiers **desert** . . .

. . . these deserters returning to their villages quicken the **decline** of SR support among the peasants.

I.G. Tsereteli (1882-1959) right-wing Georgian Menshevik and Minister in Kerensky's government.

Tsereteli, SR and other Mensheviks organize a mass demonstration to **prove** that Bolshevism has no popular support. But the 400,000 workers who march through Petrograd, June 18, 1918, come out **for** Bolshevism! Maxim Gorky reports a **complete triumph** for Bolshevism in Novaya Zhizn.

...MEANWHILE, KEEP EXPLAINING...

What is required of us is the **ability** to explain to the masses that the social and political character of the war is determined not by the 'good will' of individuals or groups, or even of nations, but by the position of the **class** which conducts the war, by the class **policy** of which the war is a continuation by the **ties** of capital, which is the dominant economic force in modern society, by the **imperialist character** of modern capitalism, by Russia's dependence in finance, banking and diplomacy upon Britain, France, and so on. To explain this skilfully in a way the people would understand **is not easy** . . .

THE JULY DAYS...

April, Lenin had to overcome the reluctant
Old Bolsheviks'. But by July he faces the
revolutionary impatience of the 'leftists'.
Leaders of the Bolshevik Military
Organization, Kronstadt sailors and the

Petrograd machine-gun regiment want an
immediate armed uprising . . .

. . . but Lenin says 'Not yet!'

THE PEOPLE MUST CONVINCE **THEMSELVES** THAT THERE ARE **NO ALTERNATIVES** TO BOLSHEVIK POLICY... WE DON'T WANT A **BLANQUIST PUTSCH!**

On July 4th another half-million demonstrators are in the streets, believing that SR-Menshevik leaders of the Soviet can be **forced** to take power . . .

TAKE POWER, YOU SONOFABITCH, WHEN IT'S **GIVEN** TO YOU!

WE **RESOLUTELY** REFUSE TO DO SO!

THE LAST THING CHERNOV & CO. **WANT** IS THE SOVIET **POWER** WHICH THE MASSE ARE TRYING TO HAND THEM

TROTSKY

Once the July Movement begins, the Bolsheviks cannot refuse to join it. "Better to suffer defeat with the masses than remain neutral!"

Until then, Lenin had argued that the left parties should agree to an immediate **peaceful** seizure of power by the Soviets while there was still time.

But on 3 and 4 July, the SR-Menshevik leadership of the Soviet virtually handed over power to the counter-revolution by summoning Cossacks to Petrograd, disarming and disbanding revolutionary regiments and workers, approving and tolerating acts of violence against Bolsheviks, introducing the death penalty at the front, etc.

The Pravda offices are wrecked, hundreds of Bolsheviks arrested, including Kamenev and Trotsky. Lenin is accused in the press of being a 'German agent'. Lenin hides out in the Razliv marshes where he continues writing . . .

> THE OVERTHROW OF THE BOURGEOISIE CAN BE ACHIEVED ONLY BY THE PROLETARIAT BECOMING THE **RULING** CLASS*...

* this is the essence of Lenin's book, **State and Revolution**, and it argues, as Marx did, for the **political rule** of the proletariat.

Can the proletariat develop its political independence ?

Capitalism began to ripen within feudal society, hundreds of years ago. The merchants, who **exchanged** commodities, grew towards independence as a **capitalist class** in opposition to a landowning feudal class.

But the merchants had **something** to work from — an autonomous base in the new, expanding cities of Europe. Here they were able to establish the material, technical and cultural foundations for the independence of their class.

But the proletariat — the mass of commodity **producers** — remained an oppressed, exploited class. Why? Because the bourgeoisie monopolized the means of production and exchange . . . and also **education**. Capitalists don't only have 'money': they have the means to create **administrative elites**. Administration is the key to controlling the means of control — without **that**, the proletariat remains a backward class in a highly developed society.

In time, the working class develops **defensive organs** — such as trade unions. But the collapse, in 1914, of the German SDP labour party was proof that it could not **deal** with a real state crisis . . . because it was not prepared for organizing all of society, for **administering** it.

Socialism does not simply 'grow out' of capitalism. To achieve socialism, a revolutionary proletarian class must **oppose** capitalism, just as the bourgeoisie once opposed feudalism by **managing** itself as an independent class.

The proletariat can develop its own administration, its own independent **socialist** economy, only if it achieves political rule. This is what Marx meant by the rallying slogan, the "dictatorship of the proletariat".

...'DICTATORSHIP OF THE PROLETARIAT` IS ONLY ANOTHER NAME FOR A **WORKERS'** STATE!

...OR A STATE WHICH FUNCTIONS AS A DIRECT **PRODUCERS'** DEMOCRACY

LENIN DISGUISED AS A FINNISH RAILWAY FIREMAN

KERENSKY GETS COLD FEET...

The German armies **advance** and on 21st August 1917 they capture Riga, an important harbour of the pro-Bolshevik fleet.

GOOD! THE GERMANS SHOULD TAKE PETROGRAD TOO!

President of the Duma Rodzianko expresses a wish of the bourgeoisie — to be rid of the Soviet!

...AND IF NOT THE GERMANS, THEN (MAYBE) A MILITARY-TAKE-OVER??

GET KORNILOV'S TO IMPOSE MARTIAL LAW

LET ME RID RUSSIA OF THE REDS AND ALL THOSE DAMN SOVIETS!

Kerensky, now Prime Minister of the Provisional Government, toys with a 'Napoleonic' plot to seize Petrograd.

Boris Savinkov, a leading SR militant and Governor-General of Petrograd is in league with Kerensky and Kornilov.

General L.G. Kornilov, appointed Supreme Commander by Kerensky, heads the 'Putsch' against the Petrograd Soviet, August 27-30.

At the last minute Kerensky gets cold feet and abandons the plot. Kornilov's military uprising was defeated in a few days by the workers and soldiers of the Petrograd Soviet — thanks to the assistance of the Bolshevik party . . . which was still being **suppressed** and **persecuted** by the government!

After Kornilov's defeat, Lenin tries **once more** to reach agreement with the SR-Menshevik leaders in the hope of setting up a workers' democracy **peacefully**.

But they reject Lenin's offer and still support Kerensky's government.

Meanwhile the mass popular shift towards Bolshevism **increases** . . .

ON SEPT. 24TH THE BOLSHEVIKS WIN 350 SEATS OUT OF 710 IN THE MOSCOW MUNICIPAL ELECTIONS!

BOLSHEVIKS GAIN THE **MAJORITY** IN THE SOVIETS OF PETROGRAD, TASHKENT, KAZAN, REVAL, KALUGA, ETC.

Trotsky elected President of the Petrograd Soviet, Sept. 25th.

V.P. Nogin, Bolshevik, elected President of the Moscow Soviet.

October 10th
The Bolshevik Central Committee declares for an armed insurrection.

October 18th
Zinoviev and Kamenev publish an **open letter** in Gorky's paper **opposing** the insurrection!

October 20th
The Bolshevik Military Revolutionary Committee prepares . . .

October 24th
Kerensky issues orders for the arrest of the Bolshevik MRC . . .

143

On the night of the 24th Lenin arrives at Bolshevik headquarters at the Smolny Institute (a former girls' school) and at 2a.m. of the 25th operations begin . . .

WE SYNCHRONIZED THE SEIZUP OF POWER WITH THE OPENING OF THE 2ND SOVIET CONGRESS ON THE 26TH.

Red Guards occupy all key points — railways, bridges, telegraph, telephone and electricity installations.

The attack on the Winter Palace, headquarters of Kerensky's government.

The government defence force of young officer-cadets offers no resistance. **No blood is shed.**

144

REVOLUTION

Women's Battalion defending the Winter Palace surrender at 9 a.m.

The ministers of the provisional government are arrested.

Kerensky flees . . .

PERFECT ORGANIZATION – THANKS TO COMRADE TROSTKY! ONLY 5 CASUALTIES IN PETROGRAD. BUT IN MOSCOW...

STALIN

In Moscow, the Menshevik and SR leaders of the City Duma organized a 'White Guard' which ruthlessly massacres workers. It took six days of bitter street-fighting before the Bolsheviks win, on Nov. 2.

'WE SHALL NOW PROCEED TO CONSTRU
THE SOCIALIST ORDER...'

Lenin's **first words** to the Congress of Soviets
on Oct. 26th (or Nov. 8th new style calendar).

The first Socialist government in the world!

The Congress elects a new Executive of the All-Russia Soviets consisting of 102 members:
62 Bolsheviks, the rest Mensheviks, SRs and others. The first **Soviet of People's Commissars**
was composed solely of 15 Bolsheviks with Lenin as Chairman.

On the morning of the 26th the Soviet abolishes the **private ownership** of land, but affirms the peasant's right to **occupy** and **work** his new holding.

THE BOLSHEVIKS HAVE **STOLEN** OUR PROGRAMME!

V.P. Milyutin, Commissar of Agriculture.

...BUT YOU ONLY **TALKED** ABOUT IT. WE'LL PUT IT INTO **PRACTICE!**

DOESN'T THIS BREAK WITH OUR OWN PROGRAMME OF **LAND NATIONALIZATION?**

Chernov, Kerensky's ex-Minister of Agriculture.

Will the peasantry act in the spirit of **our** programme or in that of the SRs? It is of little importance: the main thing is for them to have the firm assurance that there will be **no more landlords** and that they can set about organizing their own lives.

THE **REAL PROBLEM** IS — WILL WE BE LEFT IN **PEACE** TO DEVELOP SOCIALISM?

The first steps towards a **direct producers' democracy**, according to Lenin, do not seem so extreme today. He did not contemplate the **total** nationalization of heavy industry, but rather an effective workers' control and the growing partipation of the socialist state in a **mixed economy** in which capitalists would retain some place.

V.A. ANTONOV OVSEYENKO COMMISSAR OF WAR

147

THE BREST-LITOVSK PEACE TREATY

October 27th Lenin issues an appeal on radio calling for **an immediate armistice.** But in the December peace talks, the Germans demand 215 thousand square kilometres of territory (which contain **20 million people!**) and 3,000 million gold rubles!

TROTSKY LEADS THE SECOND ROUND OF TALKS IN JANUARY...

*WE CAN'T CARRY ON FIGHTING — BUT WE CAN'T ACCEPT THESE **OBSCENE** PEACE TERMS EITHER!*

*OUR AIM SHOULD BE A **REVOLUTIONARY WAR AGAINST GERMAN IMPERIALISM!***

Bukharin leads a strong 'left' opposition to peace which believes that **continued war** will encourage the outbreak of a workers' revolution in Germany.

*BUT SUPPOSE THE GERMAN REVOLUTION DOESN'T OCCUR **SOON**? WE'LL END UP IN EVEN **WORSE** SHAPE!*

To help the socialist revolution on an international scale by accepting the possibility of **defeat** of that revolution **in one's own** country is . . . unwise and **un-Marxist!**

148

Lenin was in the minority **again**! But his realism proved only too correct! The Germans advance on Feb. 18th, occupy the Ukraine and threaten Petrograd itself.

Russia was forced to accept peace, March 3rd 1918, but the German occupation lasted another 9 months till November. Meanwhile 'White' **counter-revolutionary armies** were created with German help in the Ukraine, the Don and Kuban areas. So begins the White counter-revolution which it will take **3 years to defeat!**

149

...THE BOLSHEVIKS ARE NOT A LEGAL, DEMOCRATIC GOVERNMENT...

...SO WHAT'S WRONG WITH STRUGGLING AGAINST THEM?

IF YOU HAVE THE SUPPORT OF THE PEOPLE... WHY DO YOU NEED THE GERMANS AND WHITE TSARIST GENERALS?

CHKHEIDZE

TSERETELI

Some facts about the Bolshevik 'seizure of power'...

Anti-Bolshevik propaganda has always claimed that Lenin merely 'seized power', that October was a **coup d'etat**, a conspiracy led by an undemocratic minority, etc. But the **facts** are that, throughout the summer of 1917 and after, **popular support** was shifting rapidly towards Bolshevism, and this was expressed democratically in the urban and Soviet elections across Russia.

The general elections to the new **Constituent Assembly** gave these results on December 30, 1918:

Kadets and other bourgeois parties	4,600,000 (13%)
SRs	20,900,000 (58%)
Mensheviks	1,700,000 (4%)
Bolsheviks	9,023,963 (25%)

The majority had, in fact, voted for a **revolutionary** democracy. But what did the main parties **really** stand for, by 1918?

Kadets

The party of the big bourgeoisie, even **before** October, was in favour of the military suppression of the Soviets, and by December had gone over to the 'White' pro-monarchist officers.

SRs

The party was split into opposed, **irreconcilable** factions. But it presented itself in the elections as the single "party of the peasants". The Right SRs, under Kerensky, Chernov, etc. had already engaged in anti-Soviet conspiracies. The Left SRs decided to support the October revolution only **after** its success. For a time, Left SRs participated in the government as commissars and Soviet executives. But they attempted to **seize** power in July-August, 1918.

Mensheviks

Half their vote came from the nationalist, right-wing base in the Caucasus which was non-proletarian. However, at the Menshevik Central Committee Congress, October 17-21, 1918, the leadership recognized that the Bolshevik revolution had been both **necessary** and **popularly supported**!

Bolsheviks

Their vote represents the **crucial nerve centre** of the revolution — the proletariat and over half the army and navy (i.e. **peasants** in uniform).

ONLY A **LUNATIC** CAN IMAGINE THAT THE KADET, MENSHEVIK OR SR LEADERS WERE "DEMOCRATIC"...

...AND WE WEREN'T LUNATIC ENOUGH TO PLACE THE **FATE OF THE REVOLUTION** IN THE HANDS OF THE ASSEMBLY!

ON JAN.18th 1918, SOVIET WORKERS AND SOLDIERS **DISSOLVE** THE ASSEMBLY...WITHOUT FUSS OR SENSATION.

Sverdlov President of the All-Russia Soviet Executive.

Bukharin head of the Moscow Regional Bureau.

The civil war... and the 'undemocratic democrats'

Gorky's own words in **Novaya Zhizn**, Oct. 28, 1917. But, like Plekhanov, he never engaged in **hostile actions** against Bolshevism. During the Civil War, Gorky rallied again to the support of the Soviet.

Only a **few** of the many anti-Bolshevik leaders. These people began as liberals, one-time Marxists, veteran Narodniks, terrorists, founders of the SR Party and Mensheviks. They all supported a counter-revolutionary dictatorship backed by British, US and French military intervention and conspired actively with 'White' generals to overthrow the Soviet.

x

The 'civil war' was, in fact, a **class war** which in 3½ years left the entire country in ruins. **Middle class** resistance to the Soviets came from petty-bourgeois socialists, technicians, officials and military staff.

Why didn't the socialists **cooperate** with the proletarian revolution — and save Russia from calamity?

1 The SR-Menshevik ideologists wanted a bourgeois capitalist republic in which **they** would constitute the administrative elite.

2 Mistakenly, they believed that the Bolsheviks had merely 'seized power' which they could 'seize back'.

3 'They could not believe that the proletariat, a class with 'no history', no experience of government, was the **legitimate**, democratic force of the revolution.

THE LEADING 'WHITE' GENERALS, 1918~1920

The 'White' counter-revolution, from the start, had to rely on the **non-democratic** support of the old Tsarist general staff.

GENERAL A.DENIKIN

ADMIRAL A.KOLCHAK

'ATAMAN' DUTOV

GENERAL P.WRANGEL

'ATAMAN' SEMYONOV

GENERAL N.N.YUDENICH

Denikin, Commander-in-Chief of all South Russia, was appointed Dictator of Russia by a joint Allied and White conference at Jassy, Rumania, Nov. 1918. Kolchak was proclaimed Supreme Ruler by an Allied -supported White government in Omsk, Siberia, Dec. 1918. Dutov led a Cossack army in the South Urals; and Generals Alexeyev, Krasnov and Kornilov led other Cossacks in the Ukraine, Don and Kuban regions. Semyonov led White forces on the Manchuria border and supported Japanese intervention. Yudenich prepared an attack in 1919 on Petrograd with British and Finnish support. Wrangel organized the last White army in the Crimea, 1920.

THE ALLIED INTERVENTION ⇶

Churchill, British Secretary of War in 1918, was the chief instigator of Allied military intervention. British Prime Minister **Lloyd George** was nervous that Bolshevism might 'infect' British workers. **Clemenceau**, French War Minister, wanted a quick military victory over Bolshevism. US President **Wilson** preferred diplomacy and blockades. Czech troops were promised by **Benes** in exchange for Allied recognition of Czechoslovakia's independence. **Pilsudski**, military dictator of Poland, invaded Russia with French help in 1920.

WOODROW WILSON

JOSEPH PILSUDSKI

'TIGER' CLEMENCEAU

D. LLOYD GEORGE

EDUARD BENES

BRITAIN RULES OK?

IN THE 'CIVIL WAR'...

The Allies refused to recognize the Brest-Litovsk Treaty and preferred to support a 'White' government which would continue the war. Moreover, the Bolsheviks struck a mortal blow against Allied imperialism when, on Jan. 28, 1918, they **cancelled** Russia's national debt (80,000,000,000 gold rubles or **two-thirds** the total national wealth!) which meant no repayment of foreign loans!

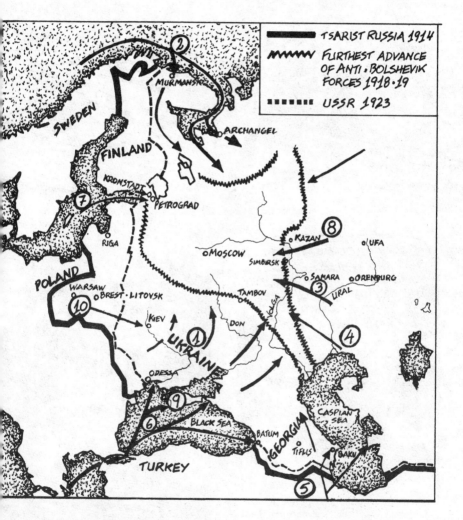

1.	Denikin, Krasnov etc. 1918-19	6.	French and British 1918
2.	British, US and Whites 1918-19	7.	Yudenich and allies 1919
3.	Czech Legions and Whites 1918	8.	Kolchak 1919-20
4.	Cossacks 1918	9.	Wrangel 1920
5.	British and Turks 1918	10.	Pilsudski 1920

'Against the Bolsheviks

On August 30, 1918, Fanny Kaplan, a Right SR assassin, seriously wounds Lenin with 3 pistol shots . . .

. . . on the same day, another SR assassin kills M.S. Uritsky, President of the Petrograd Cheka.

IT'S NO GOOD **LAMENTING** THAT THE **WHITES** EMPLOY *'UNLAWFUL'* METHODS AGAINST THE LAWFUL GOVERNMENT OF THE SOVIETS... WE MUST **DEFEND** OURSELVES!

DZERZHINSKY

The Military Revolutionary Committee of the Petrograd Soviet, which planned the October revolution, was reorganized on 7/20 Dec. 1917 as 'the All-Russian Extraordinary Commission' (**Cheka** for short) for 'combating counter-revolution and sabotage', under the presidency of Dzerzhinsky.

156

White 'Protective Corps' s

all methods are good'

r SR attempts are made against Trotsky's

V. Volodarsky, Bolshevik agitator, was killed June 20th.

Bukharin wounded in the attempt by Left SRs and anarchists to blow up Moscow Party Headquarters, Sept. 25, 1919 (12 deaths).

down Red Guards, 1918

The Civil War, 1918-20, was a time of great chaos, and estimates of Cheka executions vary from 12 to 50 thousand. But even the **highest** figure does not compare to the ferocity of the **White Terror** . . . for instance, in Finland alone, the number of workers executed by the Whites approaches 100,000!

157

The Third Communist International

Lenin expected that the October revolution would act as a 'fuse', a 'pilot-light' for revolutions in other, more **advanced** countries of the world. Russia was the **pioneer** — but she needed the help of a world socialist revolution to overcome the gigantic difficulties caused by the Civil War.

...BUT NO OTHER COUNTRY MANAGED TO REPEAT RUSSIA'S PROLETARIAN VICTORY!

BELA KUN (1886-1939)

ROSA LUXEMBURG AND KARL LIEBKNECHT

ANTONIO GRAMSCI

The 3rd Communist International was established March 2-6, 1919, during the darkest days of the Civil War. Its members didn't do very well! **Bela Kun** led the Hungarian Soviet Republic which lasted March-August 1919. **Luxemburg** and **Liebknecht** were murdered January 1919 during the Berlin workers' uprising. **Eisner**, the socialist premier of Bavaria's 'Red Republic', 1918-19, was assassinated. Noske's 'White' army suppressed the soviets in Bavaria, Bremen, Kiel and Berlin. In Italy, **Gramsci's** attempt to create a socialist 'United Front' againt Fascism failed. **Dimitrov**, Bulgarian Communist leader, escaped the savage destruction of the Party in 1923. **DeLeon**, USA Socialist Party leader, founded the Industrial Workers of the World (IWW) in 1905. The IWW, called 'Wobblies' because of their anti-war stand, were brutally persecuted in 1919.

The international revolutionary movement achieved one thing — it helped to weaken and defeat the intervention of the capitalist countries against Soviet Russia.

KURT EISNER

GEORGI DIMITROV
(1882·1949)

DANIEL DELEON (1852·1914)

159

THE RED ARMY...

Soviet Russia, without help 'from the outside', had to **create** a Red Army able to combat the combined forces of the Whites and Allied interventionists.

IN 1917, A REGULAR ARMY HAD CEASED TO EXIST!

COMMANDERS HAD TO BE FOUND AMONG INEXPERIENCED COMMUNIST WORKERS AND SOLDIERS!

WE COULDN'T HAVE FORMED AN ARMY OF A MILLION MEN BY 1919... IF THE MASSES HADN'T SUPPORTED US!

M. TUKHACHEVSKY was a 21-year-old sub-lieutenant in 1914 who commanded whole armies during the Civil War.

V. I. BLYUKHER a Bolshevik worker and N.C.O. who became one of the Red Army's best strategists.

S. M. BUDYONNY another N.C.O. who commanded the Red cavalry (made up in 1919 of Cossacks who began rallying to Bolshevism.)

The young Soviet Republic paid an enormous price for its victory. Large numbers of its best, most **politically conscious** workers perished in the fighting; the people were exhausted, the country in ruins.
In this period of **total war**, the danger of economic collapse became greater than military defeat.

TRUE, WE **WON**...
BUT THE REVOLUTION
WAS **BLED WHITE**
BY THE WHITES!

TROTSKY
appointed War Commissar, March 1918, was the inspired organizer of the Red Army.

War communism...

By 1919, the Allied **blockade** of Russia is total — nothing can get in or out. The Whites occupy the ports, 60% of railways and the key regions of industrial and grain production. Millions are threatened with starvation! **War Communism**, in the spring of 1918, is designed to meet this emergency in two ways:

1. increasing **nationalization** of industry (at much faster pace than Lenin believes wise)
2. encouraging poor peasants to assist the proletariat in **confiscating grain** hoarded by better-off Kulaks.

> Lenin said: "In conditions of crisis, shortage, loss of cattle, the peasant must give his produce **on credit** to the Soviet power for the sake of a large-scale industry which has not yet given him a thing!"

THE SPECTRE OF FAMINE AND MUTINY

But 3 years is a long time to test the patience of workers and peasants literally dying of hunger! British secret service agents, Menshevik and SR agitators provoke strikes in 1919. Serious peasant uprisings occur in 1920-21. One of these was led by **Makhno** in the Ukraine. Makhno was a partisan leader who fought the Whites, 1918-20, and tried to set up an independent anarchist federation in the Gulyai-Polye region. His refusal to merge with the Red Army led to his defeat in August 1921.

...A BUNCH OF ARMED KULAKS ON HORSEBACK!

TROTSKY'S DESCRIPTION OF MAKHNO'S ARMY

The Kronstadt sailors mutiny...

The Kronstadt Soviet, a strong island fortress with 15,000 men, demanded immediate reforms of War Communism. Their revolt, March 5-18, 1921, reflects the **peasant origins** of the Kronstadt sailors and the influence of SR and anarchist agitators. Action had to be immediate, before the ice melted and the sailors could move their battleships against Petrograd. The situation is settled by cannons and troops brought over the ice by Tukhachevsky.

while Lenin tries to meet the demands of the peasants...

If the sailors had waited, most of their 'peasant demands' would have been satisfied by the N.E.P. — **New Economic Policy** — which Lenin put forward at the Tenth Congress of the Communist Party, 8-16 March, 1921.

'It was the war and the ruin that forced us into 'War Communism'. It was not, and could not be, a policy that corresponded to the economic tasks of the proletariat. It was a makeshift. The correct policy of the proletariat exercising its dictatorship in a small-peasant country is to obtain grain in exchange for the manufactured goods the peasant needs.

We know that so long as there is no revolution in other countries, only agreement with the peasantry can save the socialist revolution in Russia.'

The N.E.P. put a stop to grain requisitions. It instituted free trade in grain, concessions to foreign capitalists, tolerance towards small traders, artisans and even small-scale industries. *163*

N.E.P. or the 'peasant Brest~Litovsk'...

The N.E.P. was, in Lenin's words, the **economic** equivalent of the Brest-Litovsk peace treaty . . . and it was opposed by the 'Left Communists' who had also resisted peace in 1918. In 1921, they defended the radical measures of War Communism, just as in 1918 they had argued for an all-out revolutionary war.

BUKHARIN   SHLIAPNIKOV, COMMISSAR OF LABOUR   KOLLONTAI

... CONTINUE THE OFFENSIVE AGAINST CAPITAL WITH *MORE* NATIONALIZATION – *MORE* EXPROPRIATION!

TRADE UNIONS SHOULD ASSUME THE DIRECT ECONOMIC *MANAGEMENT* OF PRODUCTION!

WE OPPOSE ANY RE-INTRODUCTION OF CAPITALIST METHODS OF PRODUCTION!

The N.E.P., which Lenin defined as 'State Capitalism', was not a return to 'capitalism'. Lenin had always envisaged the **temporary co-existence** of private property and communist property. " . . . you must first attempt to build small bridges which shall lead a land of small peasant holdings through State Capitalism to Socialism. Otherwise you will **never** lead tens of millions of people to Communism."

Lenin was bitterly criticized for introducing factory piece-work and the assembly-line system known as 'Taylorism' (the scientific management of industry devised by the U.S. engineer F.W. Taylor and used by Ford.)

Output of an assembly-line worker being studied in Gastyev's Bio-Mechanic Laboratory, circa 1920.

"Lenin wants to turn people into machines . . ."
Exactly the same accusation, made by Axelrod back in 1903, reveals the intellectual's fear of factory discipline and the **underestimation** of industrial labour as the basic force of social progress.

LENIN'S LAST STRUGGL

Weakened by the 1918 assassination attempt, overworked, afflicted with constant migraines, Lenin's health began to decline. In May, 1922, he suffers a stroke which leaves him partly paralyzed and unable to speak or write. By sheer will power, he managed to return to work in October.

In his last writings, again and again, Lenin hammers home the need for mass **education** as the basis for popular **self-administration**. For this reason, Lenin emphasized the importance of workers' and peasants' **cooperatives** as schools of self-management.

"Strictly speaking, there is 'only' one thing we have left to do and that is to make our people so 'enlightened' that they understand all the advantages of everybody participating in the work of the cooperatives, and organize this participation. 'Only' that. There are now no other devices needed to advance socialism. But to achieve this 'only', there must be a veritable revolution — the entire people must go through a period of cultural development."

LENIN, ON COOPERATION, 4-6 January 1923.

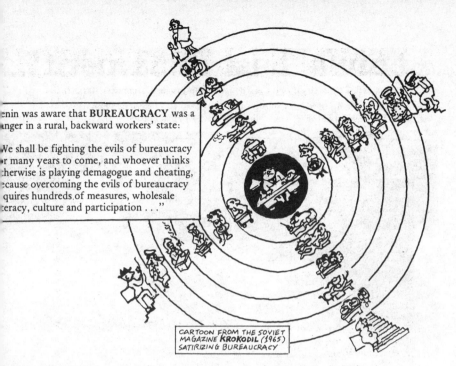

enin was aware that **BUREAUCRACY** was a
anger in a rural, backward workers' state:

We shall be fighting the evils of bureaucracy
or many years to come, and whoever thinks
therwise is playing demagogue and cheating,
cause overcoming the evils of bureaucracy
quires hundreds of measures, wholesale
teracy, culture and participation . . .''

CARTOON FROM THE SOVIET
MAGAZINE **KROKODIL** (1965)
SATIRIZING BUREAUCRACY

enin also demanded that steps be taken to protect non-Russians in the Soviet Union
rom any bullying by ''Great-Russian chauvinists'':

. . . that really Russian man, the Great-Russian chauvinist, is in substance a
ascal and a tyrant, such as the typical Russian bureaucrat is. There is no doubt that
he infinitesimal percentage of Soviet or sovietized workers will drown in that
ide of chauvinistic Great-Russian riffraff like a fly in milk . . .''

enin's hopes for international revolution, after 1919, were focussed on the colonized
ations of the 'Third World', especially Eastern ones with predominantly peasant populations. 167

Lenin's 'Last Testament'...

When Lenin died, 21 January 1924, the Russian revolution lost its greatest Marxist . . .

Lenin has left a record of his thoughts on the men capable of succeeding him. He dictated this 'Testament' on 25 December 1922 and 4 January 1923.

THE ABILITY TO **SEE STRAIGHT** WITHOUT OVERLOOKING THE TWISTS, TURNS AND ZIGZAGS OF **REALITY**... THAT IS WHAT MARXISM TEACHES!

Comrade Stalin, having become General Secretary, has concentrated enormous power in his hands, and I am not sure he always knows how to use that power with sufficient caution . . . Stalin is too rude, and this fault, entirely supportable in relation to us Communists, becomes insupportable in the office of General Secretary. Therefore I propose to the comrades to find a way to remove Stalin from that position and appoint to it another man who in all respects differs from Stalin only in superiority — namely, more patient, more loyal, more polite, and more attentive to comrades, less capricious, etc.

. . . Comrade Trotsky . . . is distinguished not only by his exceptional ability — personally, he is, to be sure, the most able man in the present Central Committee — but also by his too far-reaching self-confidence and a disposition to be far too much attracted by the purely administrative side of affairs.

Bukharin . . . may be considered the favourite of the whole Party. But his theoretical views can only with the greatest reservations be regarded as fully Marxist, for there is something scholastic in him. (He never has learned, and I think never fully understood, the dialectic.)

. . . the October episode of Zinoviev and Kamenev was not, of course, accidental, but it ought as little to be used against them as the 'non-Bolshevism' of Trotsky.

A 'MONUMENT' FOR LENIN?

BAH! MONUMENTS ONLY ATTRACT PIGEONS!

[C]RADE LENIN WAS AFRAID OF [K]NOWLEDGING [HI]S MISTAKES

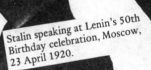

Stalin speaking at Lenin's 50th Birthday celebration, Moscow, 23 April 1920.

Cold War hostility towards Russia and the errors of Stalinism have built up a **false** image of Lenin. Readers who want to make up their **own** minds, without prejudice, should consider the following assessment of Lenin very carefully:

"When he was still alive, Lenin was not regarded as a **source** of authority — even if he possessed considerable personal authority. The latter derived from the rational force of the arguments with which he defended his opinions and political choices; from the prestige he had won by his past successes . . . nor was his authority ever considered indisputable. On the contrary, he always encountered disagreement, resistance or opposition even within the ruling group of the Bolshevik Party. He was the recognized 'head' of the Party, but it was permissible to disagree with him and, when it was thought necessary, other comrades were allowed and even expected to oppose his will. He was 'head' because he managed to convince and draw into struggle even wavering and reluctant people, not because he had the right to reject or silence opponents. Convinced of the need for firm Party discipline, he never tried to place his opponents under a discipline to which he was not himself subject. Nor did he seek to obtain within the Party a formal pre-eminence which would enable him to escape the control of the majority in any sphere of decisions." *VALENTINO GERRATANA*

Well, was it avoidable?

Conditions in Russia between 1920 and 1923 were indescribable: in the countryside, famine, typhus epidemics, revolts and banditry; in the cities, hunger, unemployment, strikes and mutinies. Something had to be done quickly to stimulate the economy and repair the deepening rift between the Party and the mass discontent with Bolshevism.

Lenin's solution was the **New Economic Policy** of 1921, another pragmatic example of his "bending the stick" or "taking one step back, two steps forward". Adoption of a limited free market economy was, however, a virtual admission that Lenin's Menshevik critics had been right – Russia was not ready for a quantum leap into fully-fledged Communism.

By 1923, 76% of retail trade was privately controlled. Most wholesale and all foreign trade went on being state managed. Industries were handed back to private owners, but the 8.5% that remained nationalized employed some 80% of the work-force, so industry was hardly "marketized" at all. A partly gold-backed rouble stabilized the currency and a new banking system controlled the money supply. Improvements were gradual but effective.

The question was – did Lenin foresee the NEP as temporary or longer-term? Lenin's response at the time seems unequivocal. "It will take at least two decades before 'socialism' arrives."

The years 1921 to 1923 are remarkable for Lenin's capacity, at the limit of exhaustion, to re-think the road to socialism. In some important aspects, Lenin showed himelf independent-minded enough not to be a "Leninist".

In his last speeches and writings, Lenin bangs on about three things. His first emphasis is on **education**, of the masses but of Communists too. "Less windy talk about 'proletarian culture', and let's rid ourselves first of a serf mentality. We could do with some solid bourgeois culture for a start."

Lenin's second aim was to encourage the speedy build-up of agricultural co-operatives, for him the obvious main road to eventual socialism in a predominantly peasant society. "Don't go talking 'communism' to the peasant," Lenin warned. "He doesn't know what you're talking about. It terrifies and alienates him."

Industrialism remains for him the mainstay vanguard of revolutionary socialist change, but he recognized how crucially it depended on the co-operation of the peasant masses to raise agricultural productivity.

Lenin's third preoccupation, and one that we have become all too familiar with in the 1990s, is the problem of nationalities and ethnic minorities. Lenin had given Stalin a free hand in 1920-21 to deal ruthlessly with the state centralization of nationalities, those especially of the Caucasus and Georgia. Suddenly, in 1922, he wages all-out war on "Russian chauvinism" and its centralist disrespect for small nations, as though – too late – he foresaw the latent dangers of nationalist ethnic conflicts.

Lenin seems to have gone full circle – from utopian origins, to scientific and organized Marxism, and back to the traditions of 19th century Russian humanism. Is it imaginable that, had Lenin lived, the Soviet regime would have gone down the road of a more practical, less dogmatic **reformist** socialism?

A reply hinges on positive and negative aspects in Lenin's own attitudes, but also on conditions finally prevailing in the last years of his life.

1. Positively, it does seem that Lenin was groping towards **politics** – a strange thing to say of someone who all of his life was nothing else but "political". Politics must be understood in a different sense than even Lenin himself had understood it until then. Lenin was looking to **govern**, and to govern according to the aims that then chiefly preoccupied him – on the basis of **culture** (education), **organization** (co-operatives) and **peace** (a federal state of nationalities). Governing in these terms is what Lenin meant by **cultural revolution**, gradually winning the confidence of the peasant masses, something very different than Mao Tse-tung's later conception of it.

2. Negatively, it is clear that Lenin was a prisoner of his own conception of the Party. He had been personally crucial in shaping the Bolsheviks as the élite strike-force of the revolution, and he ended up believing that the Party **above all** guaranteed the safety of the revolution. On this principle, he would not and could not compromise. To the end, Lenin placed his hopes in a "Communist morality" and the creation of "super-Bolsheviks" of selfless, unimpeachable rectitude. This was a dangerously élitist notion of political correctness, which would finish under the supervision of the GPU – the secret police forerunner of the KGB.

Lenin was foresighted enough to judge accurately the faults of Stalin and his other Bolshevik lieutenants, but aside from psychological finesse, his "Testament" offers no remedy except to warn the Party against the perils of a schism between Stalin and Trotsky.

Argue as Lenin could for a **politicization** of the masses, he was unable to conceive of entrusting the people **with** politics.

All of his many years abroad in exile, in various countries with democratic traditions, did not impress on Lenin any respect for "bourgeois" democracy which he considered irrelevant both to conditions in Russia and to revolutionary Marxism.

These negative aspects of Lenin's attitude begin to outweigh his last positive efforts to grope towards politics – that is, politics democratically exercised by the people.

One does not have to step outside Marxist traditions to criticize Lenin's uncompromising notion of absolute Party leadership. Antonio Gramsci (1891-1937), Italian Marxist theoretician, during his dark and mortal years of prison under Mussolini's Fascist regime, had evolved an idea of

socialist hegemony which is a reply to Lenin's Party hegemony.

By hegemony is meant the predominance of a social class over others and whose particular world view takes precedence as the dominant norm.

Gramsci asked himself the key question: how can a socialist hegemony be achieved and its world view take precedence as the dominant popular norm?

Gramsci placed his faith in the consent of the majority to isolate the minority of their oppressors. That was his vision of a socialist revolution. Gramsci's idea of revolution is therefore the struggle for winning a socialist hegemony on the basis of the **political consent** of the majority – a complete novelty in Marxist circles at that time. How did he arrive at such a maverick position?

1. Marx had concentrated chiefly on the economic analysis of capitalism. Notoriously, he left no blueprint of how socialism should or could actually function when in government.

2. Marxists thereafter were only concerned with the revolutionary moment of a **transfer of power** to socialism. What happened **after** that moment had no connection with what had gone before.

3. Marxists believed that "history" itself would bring about the transfer of power. They relied on the industrial working class to grow into an overwhelming majority that would seize power by the bullet or the ballot box.

4. Gramsci foresaw the crisis that a seizure of power would inevitably bring. The problem was not how revolutionaries came to power, but how they come to be **politically accepted** by the majority. It was not a transfer but a **transformation** of power that mattered. What is changed, what is preserved of the past? How is a revolution a fulfilment of past history, not simply a "break" with it? Failure to achieve majority consent could only arrive at a "passive revolution", the introduction of historic, economic changes from "on high" without widespread popular initiatives.

Socialist states created by Lenin, Stalin, Mao and others relied on the mechanisms of a state-managed "command" economy and excluded the mass of the people from **politics**. They failed to create socialist **societies** of democratic consent.

If you exclude the people from participation, marginalize them, threaten their identity and nationhood, you will inevitably get a **conservative response** – a Gramscian conclusion that can be drawn not only from the decline and fall of Communist regimes in the 1990s, but **all** societies, including those that embrace the free market economy because there is no apparent alternative to it.

To a limited but positive extent, Lenin understood this much in his last years when he introduced the NEP and struggled for other measures of co-operation. But he did not go further, to the extent of "politics" as Gramsci suggested. Indeed, in reality, Lenin could not have done so anyway, because by 1922 he was already marginalized by a struggle for the leadership within the Party.

The NEP was unpopular with "left" Communists and workers resentful of profiteering "Nepmen". And so, in 1928, four years after Lenin's death, when Stalin introduced the first of his **Five Year Plans**, he found considerable support. Stalin's grand schemes for accelerated industrialization, with capital appropriated from the enforced collectivization of agriculture, brought the unimaginable horrors of mass liquidations and transportations to the Gulags. These "plans" gained a short-term success at the price of the longer term total collapse of the Soviet command economy.

We can perhaps see something else now. Lenin's NEP was in certain respects an uncanny preview of Mikhail Gorbachev's attempts in the 1980s to introduce limited free market reforms to the USSR. This too was an example of "passive revolution", the stimulus of economic reform transmitted from "on high" which came too late, far too late.

The question must therefore remain open and speculative, whether or not Lenin's road of NEP **then**, in the early 1920s, uninterrupted by the "loss of Russia's greatest Marxist" and Stalin's brick-headed Bolshevism, would have led to a more flexible and enduring socialism.

Further Reading Tips

Books by Lenin

It does require more effort these days to find works by Lenin, but the 45-volume *Collected Works* in low-priced hardbacks are still available from Lawrence & Wishart, London or International Publishers, New York. Foreign Language Press, Beijing, provides a cheap selection of paperbacks, but you will have to seek them out in specialist left-wing bookshops.

Penguin paperbacks offer two Lenin classics, *What is to be Done?* (1902) and *The State and Revolution* (1918), the latter written when Lenin was on the run in 1917 and his most important contribution to the debate on international revolution. Also look out for *"Left Wing" Communism: an Infantile Disorder*, Book Marks, 1993, Lenin in polemical top form.

(Remember, when reading Lenin, that he addresses specific events in the context of Party practice. His writings do not present a systematic theory but Marxist *practice*.)

Biographies

Edmund Wilson, *To the Finland Station*, Penguin, is still the most entertaining introduction to Lenin and his revolutionary predecessors. Robert Service, *Lenin: a Political Life*, three volumes hard or paperback, Macmillan 1991, is thorough and comprehensive.

Histories

C.L.R. James, *World Revolution 1917-1936*, Humanities Press International 1993, is an excellent popular history which synthesizes the post-WWI revolutionary movements. John Reed, *Ten Days that Shook the World*, Penguin, is a journalist's classic eye-witness account of the October Revolution. Two other recommended classics are Leon Trotsky's *The History of the Russian Revolution*, Pluto Press 1985, and Victor Serge's beautiful *Year One of the Russian Revolution*, Pluto Press 1992, both by active participants. E.H. Carr, *The Bolshevik Revolution*, the first part of his 14-volume history of the Soviet Union, Penguin, remains the standard political history. If you want an economic overview, try Alec Nove, *An Economic History of the USSR 1917-1991*, Penguin. A recent study of Lenin's NEP is Alan M. Ball's *Russia's Last Capitalists: the Nepmen 1921-1929*, University of California Press paperback 1990.

Commentaries

Paul Le Blanc, *Lenin and the Revolutionary Party*, Humanities Press International 1990, is a thought-provoking reassessment. For an excellent critical history which includes a section on Lenin, consult Leszek Kolakowski's *Main Currents of Marxist Thought*, three volumes, Oxford University Press. And for those interested in Gramsci's views, try Antonio Gramsci, *Selections from the Prison Notebooks*, ed. and trans. Q. Hoare and G.N. Smith, Lawrence & Wishart 1991.

Special thanks to Philip Derbyshire at Compendium Bookshop for his helpful advice.

Richard Appignanesi is the originating editor of Icon Beginners Books, a former founder member of Writers and Readers Publishing Co-operative, the author of the best-selling *Freud for Beginners*, the fiction trilogy *Italia Pervers* and has recently completed *Made in Japan: Yukio Mishima's Report to the Emperor*, an autobiographical fiction. He is currently working on a biography the Portuguese poet, Fernando Pessoa, and is Research Associate at King's College London.

Oscar Zarate, born in Argentina, settled in London in 1971. He is an internationally acclaimed illustrator of comic strips and graphic novels. His works include: *Freud for Beginners*, *Fatlips*, a children's book with Arnold Wesker, the graphic novels of Shakespeare's *Othello*, Marlowe's *Dr Faustus Geoffrey the Tube Train and the Fat Comedian* with Alexei Sayle, *A Small Killing* with Alan Moore, and his *Mafia for Beginners* with Arnd Schneider an Richard Appignanesi (Icon Books 1994).